First 100 Days of In-home Selling

The Secret of the One-Call Close

Jim Ryerson and Ron Kahoun

W Business Books

an imprint of New Win Publishing
a division of Academic Learning Company, LLC

Published by WBusiness, an imprint of New Win Publishing,
a division of Academic Learning Company, LLC

9682 Telstar Ave. Suite 110, El Monte, CA 91731

www.WBusinessBooks.com

Cover Designed by Gary Baltazar Jr.

ISBN 13: 978-0-8329-5030-8

Manufactured in the United States of America

13 12 11 10 09   1 2 3 4 5

Library of Congress Cataloging-in-Publication Data

Ryerson, Jim.

First 100 days of in-home selling : the secret of the one-call close / Jim Ryerson
and Ron Kahoun.

    p. cm.

Includes bibliographical references and index.

ISBN 978-0-8329-5030-8 (pbk. : alk. paper) 1. Selling. 2. Direct selling.
I. Kahoun, Ron, 1963- II. Title. III. Title: First one hundred days of in-home
selling.

HF5438.25.R938 2009

658.8'72–dc22

                          2009017365

If you sell any of these 100 In-home products and services, you can benefit from the First 100 Days of In-home Selling!

Air duct cleaning

Air purification systems/ residential

Architectural Home Services (AIA - residential)

Asphalt driveways

Awnings

Barns

Basement finishing

Basement waterproofing

Bathroom remodeling

Bathtub refinishing

Boat docks

Builders - home

Cabinetry, specialty residential

Carpet and rug cleaning

Catering, home/events

Cement driveways

Central vacuum

Chimney builders/sweep/ repair

Curtainwalls, residential curtains

Decks

Deck cleaning/staining

Doors/replacement

Driveway sealcoating/repaving

Drywall services

Electrical residential

Elevators/dumbwaiters/ mobility equipment

Entry doors/security doors

Fences/fencing

Fireplaces/brick/stone/wood burning stoves

Fire damage remediation/ recovery services

Flooring

Garages

Garage doors/openers

Garage organization/cabinetry

Glass replacement/home

Golf putting greens/backyard

Gutters/Downspouts

Handyman services/carpentry

Heat pumps/alternative heating/energy systems

Holiday lighting & Decoration

Home Additions

Home gyms, exercise systems

Home improvements

Home Inspection services

Home design & planning

Home security systems

Home sound systems

Home theater systems

Hot tubs/spas/sauna

HVAC, residential

Insulation

Interior design services/
  residential
Interior lighting
Interior furnishings/design
Interior residential painting
Kitchen/remodeling
Landscaping
Lawn maintenance/fertilizer/
  mowing
Maid services
Moving/storage
Nannies/tutors – In-home
Outdoor fireplaces
Outdoor sound systems
Outside accent lighting
Post frame/pole barn
Patios/concrete
Painting exterior residential
Pavers, patio/walkway/
  driveway
Pest control/insect control
Pet fence/containment
Playground equipment
Plumbing services
Ponds/waterfalls
Pools
Pool cleaning
Power washing residential
Restoration

Roofing
Screened porches
Septic system/sewer cleaning
Shower doors/enclosures
Siding installation/repair
Sod/lawn installation
Solar energy systems,
  residential
Storage systems/home, garage
Stump grinding
Sunrooms/three-season
  porches
Suspended ceiling/tiles/
  acoustical ceiling
Tree service/removal/
  trimming
Underground lawn sprinkling
Water damage remediation/
  recovery
Weatherproofing/caulking
Well-drilling
Window cleaning
Windows/replacement
  windows/storm
Window coverings/blinds/
  draperies
Window-well covers
Wiring/central intercom/
  computer
Wood cabinets/floors/
  refinishing

Add your product/service here. If your product is not listed please contact us at www.salesoctane.com and we'll add it for the next printing!

Dedications

This book is dedicated to:

My wife, the best friend I have. Thank you for putting up with my bottomless energy, laser-like drive, and constant activity. You're the best!

My three beautiful daughters, Katherine, Elizabeth, and Anna. I learn from you every day and I am so proud of you. Continue doing what you love, and a wonderful life will continue.

My father, who taught me the discipline of integrity and hard work, and my mother, who was always optimistic—three principles required for sales success.

My father-in-law, the quintessential steady salesperson whom everyone likes. My mother-in-law who helped train up a child in the way she should go. The tradition continues.

My creator, God, who has given me everything I have, including the gift to enjoy this race called life.

—Jim Ryerson

To my wife, Amy, Thank you for your patience for putting up with my persistence to achieve and my endless drive. We have had many ups and a few downs, but you never stop believing in me.

To my two wonderful sons, Joey and Jack. I am traveling most of your young years, but it's all for you. I love you dearly.

To my father, who taught me common sense and gave me my drive. You taught me that giving up is not an option.

To God, without you all of creation does not exist. You have given me an opportunity to live in a free country and to give more after this life.

—Ron Kahoun

Contents

Step 3: Meet and Greet   69

Step 4: Visual Inspection   101

Step 10: Obtaining Referrals 213

Foreword

Our company was created over 30 years ago with a foundation based upon basic business principles. These principles start with honesty, integrity, and trust—all very important in sales. Additionally, we put the client at the top of our company's organization chart, and our goal is to act in this manner 100 percent of the time.

Additionally, since inception, we committed to being a sales organization. With this commitment, our approach was that we need to cover all bases and be detail oriented with our clients. To be successful we knew that we would have to be process oriented, and that was the beginning of our process journey.

Being successful in sales requires discipline, organization, and the ability to connect with people. These traits are especially important for **In-home** sales, where prospective customers are inviting you into their home. A salesperson who is successful at **In-home** sales needs to connect with the prospect and to possess a characteristic that the customer likes. This book gives many good tips that will help you develop these characteristics.

This book also does a superior job in taking the essential tools required to be successful at **In-home** selling and to establish an organized process that, if followed, will lead to success. The "10 Step **In-home** Sales **Continuum™**" is the ultimate outline for creating success. By following this process in detail you will be successful.

Our company utilizes the "10 Step **In-home** Sales **Continuum**™," and we have grown at the rate of almost 20 percent per year over the last 20 years. This book epitomizes the fundamentals of sales success, and the growth of our company is proof that these fundamentals work. Enjoy!!!

Sean M. Cleary
President
Cleary Building Corp.

INTRODUCTION:
How to Use This Book

To gain the most benefit from this book, read one chapter a day. The book is set up to begin on a Monday (Day 1) and continues for five days, through Friday, with the step-by-step approach of the 10-Step **In-home** Sales **Continuum™**. The subsequent two days (Days 6 and 7) offer specific guiding principles for sales professionals and will revive, renew, and inspire you on your weekend. The weekend days are called "**In-home** sales mantras." The balance of the book follows the same five days of sales process and two days of inspiration. Each day you will learn the material, do some exercises, and develop positive selling habits. Take the time to write notes, highlight key lessons, and follow through by implementing each technique on your next sales call. It won't take long. Best of all, you'll have the foundation and the framework for a successful and rewarding career selling in the home. It's a great way to start the day!

DAY 1
There Is No Sales Career
Like an In-home Sales Career

You are now in Day 1 of a 100-day journey. By Day 100 you will have learned, practiced, taped, and rehearsed several selling techniques. I (Ron Kahoun) have waited over 19 years to write this book. A majority of this book was written from notes I have kept and my experience over the last 19 years in the **In-home** sales environment. Following are key points of what makes the **In-home** sales career different from other sales positions.

We have a greater sense of urgency. With **In-home** sales, we need to get the prospects out of the market as fast as possible. Out of the market meaning they are buying from us and they are not getting more bids or proposals. We want them out of the market due to the fact that our odds of making the sale are greatly reduced if the prospect is out getting more bids. Unlike business to business (B2B) sales, where the sale may take months or even years, the **In-home** sales should close in one appointment. We know that if we don't close the sale the first time in, our competitor will most likely be coming in right behind us, and the sale is in jeopardy.

We meet with more people per day than any other sales position. In this career it is very likely that you will see at least two to four prospects per day, and you may be meeting prospects seven days a week. I recently had an event for a company that had its **In-home** sales representatives working six leads per day.

We experience more ups and downs in a day. Because of all the people we see in a day, pretty much anything can happen. We have situations such as:

- No credit, therefore we can't close out the sale.

- You made a sale, and the next day the customer wants to cancel because someone at work said they got it cheaper.

- Customers change their minds midstream.

- You made a sale, but the customer lost his/her job or got laid off and rescinded the deal.

- Installers messed up the job, and now you can't collect the final payment.

- You may have product back-orders.

- Permits weren't obtained so the sale is cancelled.

- You lost a sale, and it was the one to make a bonus or a spiff.

You must be mentally prepared for this because we guarantee anything and everything will happen.

We experience more rejection. We take more rejection than any other sales career. It's very likely that most prospects will get three to five bids for a project. You don't know if you are the first or last in. We guarantee that you will get more "nos" than "yeses." We are preparing you now, so don't get flustered when you have dry spells. We sometimes call this sophomore slump.

We live in a car. Because of all the activity, we live in our cars. We run new leads, we prospect, we conduct routine job visits, and, mostly likely, we collect final payouts. We suggest getting a CD player in your vehicle and start listening to sales training tapes. It's the best therapy for your career.

We work odd hours. We work nights and weekends. When you're selling in the home you need to be at the appointment when *all* decision makers are present, which means nights and weekends.

We have freedom. Working evenings and weekends often leaves the middle of the day open. This freedom is one of the great benefits of **In-home** sales. Manage that freedom well and you will be both rich and content.

We are entrepreneurial. We once read that selling has the highest rate of return with the smallest amount of initial investment. In other words, you can start a job on Monday, make your first sale, and have a commission for $1,500. What risk did you have to take to get that $1,500? Did you have to pay for advertising, or a building, or hire staff? Did you need to get a small business loan? All you need to do is read this book and have the will to win and you will be making money without an upfront financial investment. The sky is the limit, and you get to set that limit.

We have unlimited earning potential. We saved the best part for last: MONEY! You have *no* limit to what you can earn per year in an **In-home** sales career. The more you make, the more money your owner will make, so he or she will not cap your income.

DAY 2
Preparation: Get Going Early!
Read, Plan, and Restore

Sales is one of the most rewarding careers due to the opportunities and independence it provides. It is one of the highest-paid professions and offers greater independence than any other occupation.

The rewards, income, and independence all begin with a quick start. Your clients and prospective clients are typically available early and late in the day. If you get going early you will have the opportunity to talk to more prospects than your competitor. Decide what "early" is for you and set a goal to meet that expectation each and every day. Take your planner, PDA, or electronic calendar and mark it in every morning to read, plan and restore.

Take a few minutes of this early time to read this book, plan, and restore your energy. Reading is one of the key differentiators between those who accomplish great things and those who don't. The average person reads less than two books per year. Your commitment to reading this book places you ahead of the pack.

Keep in mind that the discipline of starting early and beginning with reading should be a lifelong habit. In 100 days, you'll be completely done with this book. Then find another book on sales and read that during your early hours. You can download my recommended reading list free at www.salesoctane.com (be sure to click "In-home" at the web site). We frequently add books to the list so you may want to pencil this activity in your planner every few months to check the list.

You'll learn more about planning later. However, for the duration of this book, review the goals of each day to make sure you accomplish the tasks in this book. They are the most important steps to ensuring success, so place them at the top of the list. Whatever the foundation in your life, we recommend taking a few minutes for an early morning ritual to reflect on that foundation. This adds perspective to the day and gives you the strength you will need when you encounter obstacles.

Now that you have read the Foreword, Introduction, and Day 1, continue with your existing sales activities. If selling is what you're meant to do, you are going to have the time of your life. Enjoy!

DAY 3
Why In-home Salespeople Fail and What to Do about It

Listed here are the top challenges faced by the **In-home** salesperson. Read each one and write down what you are going to do to make sure you do not fall into the trap of any of these challenges. Our goal in this book is to address each of these challenges and provide you with proven techniques and processes to help you become an **In-home** sales pro and avoid each of these pitfalls.

1. Lack of a selling system; therefore each appointment is a free-for-all.

   So what should you do?_____

2. No written goals for themselves.

   So what should you do?_____

3. No time management skills and no willingness to learn how to manage their time.

   So what should you do?_____

4. No understanding of their own behavioral style let alone learning to identify the prospect's behavioral style and how they should adapt on the sales call.

   So what should you do?_____

5. Prospecting and networking is of no interest to them. They do not get out and meet new people.

   So what should you do?_____

6. Not getting in front of enough qualified people (prospects). As a result, they get behind on their sales quotas and cannot catch up.

   So what should you do?_____

7. Not asking enough questions or conducting a proper needs analysis.

   So what should you do?_____

8. Not presenting their product or service properly. They are unwilling to practice in front of a video camera and review their presentation skills.

   So what should you do?_____

9. Lack of confidence in their product or pricing. They don't build or deliver value to the prospect.

   So what should you do?_____

10. Not knowing how to close. They do not commit to memory all the closing techniques and closing questions.

    So what should you do?_____

11. Can't handle rejection.

    So what should you do?_____

12. Don't uncover or handle a prospect's objections in a proper manner. They refuse to practice the objection responses provided by their company and included in this book on Day 73.

    So what should you do?_____

13. After starting to use a proven selling system they get comfortable and begin to skip steps or take short cuts.

So what should you do?_____

14. They do not continue their sales education. They don't invest time finding new ways to improve their sales skills after they start becoming successful.

So what should you do?_____

DAY 4
Goal Setting for the
In-home Sales Professional

When thinking of a great career, such as being a professional sales rep selling in the home, having written goals is a must. The ideas you learn today will help you overcome challenge No. 2 from Day 3. You can follow these guidelines:

All goals need to be in writing. This list of goals is typically set near the first of each year. Your goals need to be with you at all times; a good place could be your journal or Day-Timer. Pull these goals out and review them at least once per week; you need milestones to see if you're on track and what adjustments you need to make.

Create short-term goals that would be completed within a one-year time frame. Break them all the way down, if you like, into weeks and months. Long term can be 5, 10, and 15 years. For example, set a long-term goal for your retirement fund, college funding, and maybe that retirement cabin on the lake you have been dreaming about.

Make sure these goals are attainable. We have met many people that became depressed because year after year they never got close to their goals. For example, if you made an average of $90K over the past three years, don't set a goal for year 4 to be $275K, because this goal is most likely not attainable.

When writing out these goals make sure you are specific. By specific we mean clearly defined and measurable. If you can not measure it then how will you know when you achieve it?

Have milestones and check points in place. Measure by the day, week, month, and year your progress in achieving the goal. We suggest if you use a software program like Act, Outlook, or an on-line program such as salesforce.com that you place your check-points in your calendar with reminders.

Make sure that when a goal is reached, replace it with another. Stretch yourself, aim high but make it attainable. Athletes are great at this because they know if they can run a mile in 5:03, there has to be a way through better training to get to 5 minutes flat.

Visualize how you will reward yourself. We love visuals, such as a picture of a Corvette or of a three-season room you might want to add to your home. Place these pictures around the house, your office, and even in your Day-Timer. Maybe set the picture as a background on your laptop. Share them with your family.

Now for the best part, go get the goal. There is nothing wrong with wanting a new shiny Corvette or Porsche. When you achieve the goal, go get it! After you achieve, you will want to set more goals for the future, simply because you can see that it's attainable.

DAY 5
Value Your Time from the Start

As you begin this journey of sales you will find there will be no shortage of people, problems, opportunities, and tasks begging for your time and attention. One of the ways to stay focused is to recognize the incredible value of every minute of your time. This exercise will help you make better decisions when someone or something begins to beg for your time, or worse, you procrastinate and start to lose valuable minutes.

Follow these six tips and make sure to complete all six today.

1. *Write down how much you want to make in the next 12 months.* Don't aim low! What would you need to make in order to feel fulfilled and content in your role? We'll use an example of $100,000.

2. *Identify how many days you will work.* There are 52 weeks a year and seven days a week, and the average sales person has 13 holidays and 15 days of vacation. Add your holidays and vacation days up and subtract the number from 365.

   Example: 13 holidays and 15 days of vacation equals 28 subtracted from 365 equals 337 days to earn your goal from No. 1.

3. *Protect your personal time.* The **In-home** sales profession is one of the most high-pressure roles, in which you are "on-call"

and thinking about business at all times, day and night. As a result you need to take time to restore your energy in order to stay in top form. It's important to protect your personal time; therefore, for the purposes of this exercise we recommend protecting two days a week. Two days per week times 52 weeks a year equals 104 days of personal time. If you want to modify that amount because you plan to work less or more days per week, simply modify the amount and subtract it from the result in No. 2.

Example: Two days per week times 52 weeks a year equals 104 days subtracted from 337 (from No. 2) equals 233 available days to earn your goal from No. 1.

4. *Stay focused.* According to the Bureau of Labor Statistics, the average workday is 8.335 hours.[1] Because this is an average you will have to decide on your own number. Take the number of hours per day you will remain a focused **In-home** sales professional and multiply that number by the number of days from No. 3.

Example: 8.335 hours per day times 233 days (from No. 3) equals 1,942 available hours to earn your goal from No. 1.

5. *Figure what you are worth every single minute.* The last step is to take your income goal from No. 1 (e.g., $100,000) and divide it by the available hours to get your hourly worth. Finally, divide that hourly number by 60 to get your worth every single minute.

Example: $100,000 divided by 1,942 equals $51.49/hour divided by 60 (minutes/hour) equals $.85 per minute.

---

1   United States Department of Labor, Washington DC 20212 – Table 4. Average hours worked per day, 2005 Annual Averages. http://www.bls.gov/news.release/atus.t04.htm.

6. *Take a look at how you are spending each minute of each working day.* The goal of this exercise is to reinforce the incredible value each minute of each day so you can focus on sales-related tasks. We recommend you print out a very small label with your value per minute (example: $.85) and tape it in four places:

- Your cell phone/PDA. When a call, text message, or e-mail comes in, you can ask if you really want to take that call right now. Do you really want to stop what you are focused on doing and decrease your efficiency?

- Your office/home phone. Similar to your cell phone/PDA, you want to be aware of the value of every minute of your time as you reach for the phone.

- Your computer screen/planner. This could be your laptop, desktop, or wherever you receive e-mails and manage your calendar. When you receive the e-mail, do you really want to address it right now?

- Your speedometer. When you jump behind the wheel after agreeing to "stop by" on what you realize is a poorly qualified opportunity, you will be guilted when you see what you are worth every minute! Perhaps you should reschedule when you are going to be out on another call in the area. Those high-priority tasks sit dormant while you are in traffic. Manage your commitments!

Take 15 minutes today to calculate the value of every minute of your time and put those reminders where they will make a difference. Don't exchange your valuable dollars for a dime here or there!

DAY 6
In-home Sales Mantra No. 1:
Feel and See the Rewards

This week was a special one for me because I had a rare chance to coach an 8-year-old salesperson. This particular person is special to me as it is my son, Joey, who had his first major sales task this past week. Joey started Cub Scouts recently and was enticed when he saw a poster showing all of the rewards he could earn if he sold a certain amount of popcorn. If he sold over $250 worth, he would get a cool outdoor survival kit. In his eyes this was easy. All he had to do was knock on the door, in his cute little Cub Scout uniform, and they would run for the checkbook. Joey started his first week while I was away on a sales training assignment in Ohio. When I returned I was curious to see his progress. What happened next is a great learning lesson for all of us. You see, while I was gone Joey found his sales were coming fast and furious, meaning easy, because he knocked on the doors of people who knew our family. And, of course, they bought from him out of obligation. However, those sales were not enough to get the expensive reward he wanted, so now the fun began.

I asked if I could ride my bike and observe his selling approach. As we were riding down the street I asked Joey for his actual script. He shared with me that he would walk up to the door (of a family friend) and say, "I am selling popcorn for Troop 336. Want to buy some?" I asked Joey if he was open to influence from me and he replied that sales were up and he didn't want to make a change. So I let him go to door to door in a neighborhood many blocks away, where no one knew us, and he had 31 doors shut in his face (gently, but they were still shut). Then Joey had a bright idea—let's go to a neighborhood that had more expensive homes because they certainly would have more money and the sales would come easy. We rode our bikes a few miles, and more doors were closed in his face so he came up with another idea. Let's go to the retirement housing area because they love little kids and popcorn. Again, more closed doors. Joey was upset and wanted to quit. I sat on the curb and asked again if I could help with the script, and he finally relented and said he was open to influence.

I said let's be a bit warmer and then show all the pictures of popcorn. Try this: "Hi, I am Joey Kahoun and I live nearby. I represent Cub Scouts Troop 336, and we are promoting popcorn and would appreciate your support. Here are some of the options." Now, of course, he resisted and thought it was begging and way too long a script, but I asked him to try and see the results. We role-played the script several times, and each time he did a little better, and I kept telling him how good he sounded. He practiced the new script with me about two dozen times. In the next 15 houses he made six sales, which is almost a 50 percent close ratio.

You can follow these points:

- Set the rewards and reach for them. If you reach the one you were hoping for, then reach higher.

- Change your approach or script if need be. Don't be stubborn. Be open to influence from a coach or trainer.

- Don't give up; it's all a numbers game.

- It does not matter if you go to the rich, poor, or retired; they are all prospects.

DAY 7
In-home Sales Mantra No. 2:
Believe to Succeed

This mantra is so important because if you believe you can succeed on the inside, then you will look like an achiever on the outside. You have to look in the mirror every day and say, "I know I can succeed." When you roll up to a driveway, you must say: "I am going to make them happy customers and they are going to buy from me. I have great products and I have great service." Because you are trained and prepared to handle all objections, you need to tell yourself you are prepared to overcome every obstacle thrown at you. You have to believe you will close the sale. You have to be confident in your abilities and believe the prospect will buy from you.

Visualize something positive happening at every stage of your sales call *before* you make the sales call and you will succeed. If you don't believe in yourself, who will? For today, make a list of your strengths and weaknesses. Write down what you need to learn from this book to be a better closer and salesperson.

DAY 8
Know Yourself, Part 1

The ideas you learn today will help you overcome challenge No. 4 from Day 3: not knowing your behavioral style or your prospect's behavioral style. People buy from people they like. If you are buying a candy bar at the local convenience store you probably don't care if you like the person behind the counter. You buy the candy bar and move on. However, when people have a choice of who to buy from and if they want to let someone into their home, they will buy from someone they like versus someone they dislike. This makes sense, and most **In-home** salespeople understand this concept and work diligently at being friendly and liked by their customers. However, potential customers are also more inclined to buy from someone who is similar to them. We refer to this similarity as *behavioral style.* You have a particular behavioral style, and so does your potential customer. The way customers make their decisions is influenced by their behavioral style.

For the next several days we will be touching on the concept of how prospects make decisions and how we can modify our approach to make it easier for them to buy from us versus our competitor. Think about it this way. When I decide to buy something, I am quite impulsive. I recently bought a car over the Internet. After looking for a particular model, I found a few cars matching my criteria. Those particular cars were selling fast, and the first two I called about were sold within the next 24 hours.

As a result, I bought the third car that met my criteria over the phone, with a simple deposit on my credit card and without having viewed the car in person or even test driving the vehicle. The car was in another city so I purchased a one-way plane ticket to the city where it was located and drove it home.

You might be aghast at the thought of making a sizeable purchase without doing a lot of research. Many of you would review information online about the model you were looking to purchase, go to several automobile dealerships, evaluate several vehicles, drive them, look at the history of the car, and so forth. Some may even think it's reckless to make a major purchase in this manner and that's the point. It was not reckless for me, but it is for others. People make buying decisions differently and in some cases very differently. Unfortunately, many salespeople never realize the way *they* make buying decisions is often different from how a prospect will decide.

Issues such as the amount of information or analysis required, the level of suspicion or trust, impulsiveness or lack thereof, the speed in making a decision, and the level of emotional engagement in a purchase are just a few of the ways that people differ in how they make decisions. The unknowing salesperson will approach every prospect with the same type and quantity of information, the same "lines," the same follow-up, and the same close. With some prospects they win and with some prospects they lose. You could get more business, faster, at higher margins, *and* position yourself better for the referral by understanding how the prospect makes decisions from a behavioral standpoint and then adapting your approach to fit his or her style.

Incidentally, maybe you are asking the question, "How often is the behavioral style of the prospect different from my behavioral style?" It can be as high as 75 percent of the time, which means you may only have a 25 percent chance that the prospect behaves just like you when making a decision. Those are not good odds. The goal of these next few days is to understand your behavioral style and how you come across to your prospects and customers and then how to identify your prospect's behavioral style. We will give you a general idea to adapting your approach on Day 15, and then later in the book (Days 24 on) we go into greater detail with how to prepare for each style, what to do during the sales call with each style, and how to follow up after the sales call with each style. In some cases the approach will be very different from the way you currently "sell," and in some cases it will be similar. However, before we look at the prospect's style and how to approach him or her, we want to make sure you know your behavioral style. Our organization uses a tool available through Target Training International. You can get more information at our website, www.salesoctane.com (click on the In-home link). There are two options to help you identify your sales behavioral style.

1. You can take an online assessment by going to www.salesoctane.com and selecting the In-home link and following the directions for assessments. This online assessment will not only provide you with your exact behavioral style but will also give you 20-plus pages of insight into how you present yourself to others, how you respond to stress when selling, and how you adapt yourself, plus a review of your strengths and areas for improvement as an In-home salesperson.

2. You can go to Day 16 and follow the same methodology we use to identify a prospect's behavioral style.

Note: Three important reminders if you take the online assessment: (1) This will require 10 to 15 minutes of uninterrupted time (once you start, please make sure you finish the assessment in a single sitting). (2) Answer the questions as you are and not how you wish you could be or not how your manager would want you to answer. If you answer honestly you will have a very clear indication of how to improve your approach to get additional business. The only style that is bad for selling is the one you don't know. (3) Once you complete the assessment online you will immediately receive a copy of the results. Please have someone that has known you for some time read the overview of your results (typically the first two to four pages) and ask him/her the following question: "How accurate do you think this is?" Oftentimes you may feel like it is 80 percent accurate but someone close to you will say it's 95 to 100 percent accurate. Be prepared to learn!

DAY 9
Know Yourself, Part 2

If you have taken the assessment, this is a review of the information. If you have not taken the assessment, then identify your style from the simple steps in the following list, which is similar to how you will identify the style of a prospect or customer, as will be noted in Day 16. The reason we feel strongly you should take the assessment online is that most people are a blend of two or more styles, and the online assessment reconciles that blending of multiple styles, giving you a more accurate view of your behavioral style.

From a sales perspective, there are four behavioral styles:

1. Dominant/driver (D)

2. Influencer/expressive (I)

3. Steady/amiable (S)

4. Compliant/analytical (C)

Although most people are a blend of behavioral styles, we are going to review the individual styles as if the person were 100 percent Dominant/driver, Influencer/expressive, Steady/steadiness, or Compliant/analytical. Answer these two questions:

1. Are you an extrovert or an introvert? If you are not sure, then ask someone else what they think you are.

2. Are you more task and detail oriented, or are you more people oriented? Again, if you are not sure, ask someone else what he/she thinks you are.

Now, based on the answers to these two questions, you can arrive at a reasonable indication of your dominant behavioral style. Here's how the responses lead to figuring out your style:

D	C	Task/detail oriented
I	S	People oriented
Extrovert	Introvert	

If you are extroverted and task and detail oriented, you have a Dominant/driver behavioral style. If you are extroverted and people oriented, you have an Influencer behavioral style. If you are introverted and task and detail oriented, you have a Compliant style. If you are introverted and people oriented, you have a Steady behavioral style.

This simple two-question approach does not take into consideration the blending of two or more styles. Therefore, the list of how each style approaches decisions may change depending on your unique style. The online assessment recognizes the blending and provides a more accurate and complete list of your unique characteristics.

The following lists each behavioral style's decision-making process:

- Dominant/driver—decisive, impatient, responsible, takes calculated risk, competitive.

- Influencer/expressive —impulsive, makes the popular choice, emotional, trusting, enthusiastic.

- Steady/amiable—consistent (with past decisions), patient, little emotion, deliberate, safe.

- Compliant/analytical—cautious, careful, exacting, detailed, systematic.

Identify your behavioral style(s) and move to the next day.

In-Home Sales Continuum™

Beginning today you will begin the process known as the 10-step In-home Sales Continuum™. The graphic above illustrates the steps and the remainder of this book provides the content behind each step. The 10-step In-home Sales Continuum ™ is a proven selling system for each and every type of in-home sale. It's also a great tool for a business owner or sales manager to help a new or struggling salesperson. The steps must be followed in order and your sales success relies on completing each step.

Please feel free to contact us at www.salesoctane.com with any concerns or questions with the 10-Step In-home Sales Continuum ™

DAY 10
Step 1: The Lead

The key to the 10 Step **In-home** Sales **Continuum**™ is completing each step in sequence. You only move to the next step if the prior step has been completed. The first step is the lead—a name and a number. Steps 2 through 10 are useless without a name and a number to begin your sales process. Without a lead you are out of business.

There are five ways to get a name and a number of a prospect:

1. Company-provided

2. Prospecting

3. Networking

4. Orphans

5. Referrals

Company-Provided

In my 20 plus years of **In-home** selling/training and coaching, every company has provided leads. How the leads are generated varies from company to company. The obvious sources are newspaper ads, Internet, mailers, yellow pages and television. Each of these cost your company money. Value company-provided leads, as every sale you generate with a company-provided lead will reinforce to your employer that you value their investment in lead generation. If you really want to become a rainmaker for your company, create a sale out of every lead you receive. Consider them gifts and follow these three tips:

1. *Never complain about leads from your company.* There are bad leads at every company across the country. Your job is to turn them into good leads and keep the positive momentum flowing.

2. *It requires more than company leads to hit your income or sales goal.* The other four lead sources are essential to grow your business and create **In-home** sales wealth.

3. *Put prospecting goals in place.* Any prospecting system must have daily and weekly goals in place. A good example would be to say, "I am not going home tonight unless I make a minimum of five contacts today," or "I am not going golfing this Sunday until I have met my weekly goal for new contacts." Go back and review the goals you set in Day 4 of this program. Top sales professionals plant their seeds early so that when company leads are slow, their own leads will kick in and keep them in business. Remember, *activity* creates *productivity*.

Prospecting

If you are selling a product or service that involves exterior products, such as decks, fencing, painting, room additions, or siding/roofing, then use the "I'm worried about you" approach to prospecting.

After you make a sale, go to every neighbor near the first customer, across the street, on each side and even those two or three doors down. Knock on each door and say "Hi, I am Ron Kahoun with XYZ Decking, and my crews are installing a new deck across the street at the Jones' residence. I wanted to drop off my business card with my cell phone number on it in the event any debris blows in your yard or you experience any problems during our construction. If this occurs, please call me and I will personally come over on my day off and clean up your yard. XYZ Decking is a professional and thorough company and we want to make sure everyone is happy."

At this point they will typically thank you, and they have your card! They occasionally wonder what the Jones are getting. In an effort to keep up with the Jones, they may even inquire specifically about the project and the cost. At this point, you tell them you are on a tight schedule but that you will drop off a brochure and would be happy to stop by later and chat. The key is to avoid pitching your products or services while standing there. You want to stir up interest and set a follow-up appointment (Step 2 of the 10 step **In-home** Sales **Continuum™**). Congratulations, you just created a lead!

DAY 11
Networking, Orphans, and Referrals

Networking

As you increase your network you will increase your net worth. Networking is money. The ideas you learn today and in the future will help you overcome challenge No. 5 from Day 3: getting out and meeting new people.

Here are some great ways to network:

- Become an expert in your field and mail out a monthly newsletter. Start collecting names and e-mail addresses.

- Join clubs and associations. Become an active member of a committee so you are more connected. The best committees are membership and events. The membership committee is usually the first contact with members and everyone loves the people in the center of the events.

- Ask if you can be a speaker at your next local Chamber of Commerce, Rotary, Lions Club, or other business/social network.

- If you work with subcontractors, get their names and numbers.

- Write articles and place them on the Internet (see Ezinearticles.com for examples).

- Start your own web page. The cost usually is only $9 to $12 per month and the web host provides the software that makes it easy to create a web page. Place "before" and "after" pictures of your projects and a listing of satisfied customer testimonials after securing the approval of your client. Your company may even pick up the tab.

- Join social networking sites like linkedin.com and facebook. com. This is a free service to connect with others who might need your services or are willing to refer you to others.

- Support local charities. Whatever you give in money and time, you will get back double.

Orphans

Every company has turnover and this represents another lead source. If you are replacing a sales representative who is no longer with your company, make sure you review all of his/her open files and past customers—that is, "orphans." Follow up or visit past customers and say you're the new representative in town and you want to make sure they are happy. If they are happy with your products, then go to the referral script noted on Day 86 and ask for names and numbers of people who might also need your product or service. You will be surprised how many prospects will say, "I was wondering when someone was going to call back. The other salesperson stopped by or called and never followed up." The sales representative you replaced probably was let go because of his or her lack of sales or because he/she quit, and you can capitalize on his/her lack of professionalism by calling back.

What if the customer is irritated with the previous salesperson? What should you do if the orphan customer says, "Well, I would like to see you, but I am not happy that no one got back to me. I get the impression your company is not professional." In this case, simply reply, "Mr./Mrs. Prospect, I know exactly how you feel. I would feel the same way. May I ask you a question? If you were the president of my company, what would you have done with that salesperson that did not call you back?" The prospect will typically say, "I would have canned him ASAP!" Then you respond with "I had a feeling you were going to say that, and that's exactly what the owner of our company did. At XYZ Decking we are professional, and we provide a great product with superior service. That's why I came to work here. I would like the opportunity to correct your bad past experience because you are now my account."

By letting prospects voice their opinions you give them authority and you end up reinforcing their views by telling them you did exactly what they would do. Orphans are a great source of lead activity. Be sure to call on all open leads as well as past customers. First and foremost, before you call the orphan lead, sit back and review the data. Make sure you review the entire folder and if the prospect has received any pricing from the sales rep you replaced, make sure the pricing is current. The last thing you want to do is to get the prospect excited and have your pricing too low due to labor and material increases.

Below you will find a sample script for calling an orphan lead.

You: "Hello, is John available?"

Prospect: "This is John."

You: "John, this is Ron Kahoun with XYZ Decking. I have replaced Tim Wilson and noticed he had visited you on June 16th, is that correct?"

Prospect: "Yes, I believe so."

You: "Great, John, let me ask you, are you still in the market or have you purchased a new deck?"

If they say they made a purchase, send a thank-you card and move on. Also find out for marketing purposes who they bought from and why. If you are real good, find out what they paid for it and if they were happy with the service rendered. This will help you in the future selling against this company.

Prospect: "No, we have not decided yet."

You: "I understand, John, let me ask you, it's been four months since Tim's visit, may I ask the reason why you are still in the marketplace?"

Prospects typically respond in one of three ways:

1. "We need to get the money." In this case try to reset a second appointment and tell them about your exciting affordable financing program.

2. "We decided we really don't need a deck." In this case find out what their thoughts are and try to set a second appointment to share about a super sale coming up.

3. "We can't decide if we want a wood deck or brick patio." In this case try to set a second appointment and share the advantages of why a deck is the way to go. For instance, perhaps the salesperson you replaced did not do a good job of overcoming that objection.

If you call on leads and they say, "We're not interested," make sure you ask if they know anyone else that would be interested in your product or service. You need to make sure you qualify the lead, which we will cover in Step 2 of the **In-home** Sales **Continuum**™.

Referrals

Referrals have a much higher closing ratio than the other methods. Compared to company-provided leads, networking, and prospecting, the referral will fly through the sales process!

If you recently completed a project and want to turn that sale into guaranteed referrals, then jump to Day 85, where we cover referrals for the **In-home** sales professional in greater detail.

DAY 12
Step 2: Setting the Appointment and Prequalifying

One of the key components in the 10 Step **In-home** Sales **Continuum**™ is setting the appointment. This step must go beyond simply setting the appointment and will include both prequalifying the prospect and managing your time more effectively. Starting today, the ideas you learn will help you overcome challenge No. 6 from Day 3: not having enough qualified prospects. Here are three key points to remember:

1. *Move inquiries at the speed of sound.* If you have an assistant or call center, make sure you have a process in place for them to notify you of inquiries within minutes of receiving the call from a prospective customer. With today's technology, this should be easy. With hand-held PDAs, e-mail, text messaging, paging, and a cell phone, you should be able to get the information within minutes of receiving the inquiry. Companies that value sales will organize their operations around moving a potential sale to the front of the line.

2. *Call back within a few hours of receiving the inquiry.* You won't believe how many times I have made a sale in my **In-home** sales career and the customer will say, "Ron, I was really impressed with how fast you got back to us the first time I

called. As a matter of fact, I am still waiting for the other guy to return my call." The first key is to return a new inquiry phone call within 2 hours, period. There are two reasons why **In-home** salespeople do not respond within hours of receiving an incoming call: (1) They are full of fear; and/or (2) they are disorganized.

Get organized and make the call!

Note: Our clock starts when the inquiry comes into your company through the phone, Internet or a walk-in (if you have a showroom) and not when you receive the lead. For an **In-home** sales team to achieve sales greatness the entire organization and sales experience must be marshaled around speed. If it takes a day or two to receive an incoming lead, you are already digging yourself out of a deep hole. On the other hand, if you contact potential customers within a few hours of them inquiring about your product or service, you will leave your competition digging themselves out of a hole! Someone is going to be in the hole— make sure it's not you!

3. *Be positive.* Use positive statements such as the following:

- "Thanks so much for calling."

- "I hope I've gotten back to you quick enough." (This also reminds them of the fact they have not heard from your competitor.)

- "I hope you're enjoying this beautiful day" (if, in fact, it is beautiful out).

People appreciate and would prefer to speak with someone who is pleasant. We are not advocating a motivational approach but rather a pleasant and positive approach to this first impression.

DAY 13
In-home Sales Mantra No. 3:
Don't Judge a Book by Its Cover

Don't prejudge a lead when you view the house or the person. All top sales representatives turn the name of any home or person into some sort of positive opportunity. Even if you execute the 10 Step **In-home** Sales **Continuum**™ perfectly and the prospects just can't afford you, ask them who they may know who can afford your product or service. You will be amazed how many people have money but look like they have been broke for a lifetime.

Years ago I was a sales rep for a nationwide home improvement company in Illinois. This company specialized in kitchen cabinet refacing and countertop installation. It was a typical Friday and I had lunch with a coworker, who had shared a story with me. About three to four weeks prior, she ran a lead in Chicago. Upon her arrival she was about to knock on the door when she noticed a bad odor. She was let into the condo and no sooner did she take her first step into the room that she saw a pure dump—garbage bags stacked and rotten food on the floor and countertop. She was overcome with the smell of filth. Because the outside of the building and all of its hallways looked great, no one would have imagined what was inside this place. In her disgust, she decided to blow this lead off and get out fast.

Later in the week she mentioned her experience to a veteran sales representative at her company. He asked her for more details and if she would mind if he stopped by and spoke to the contact. She replied, "Be my guest and good luck trying to sell her anything." He made his visit, asked numerous questions, did a professional visual inspection, and sold the customer a complete kitchen, granite countertop, and custom desk to match—on the first visit. He even arranged for garbage pickup and new appliances in the deal. He set a company record for the highest paid-out commission in company history.

Later we found out that the customer was unable to clean due to a recent physical limitation. It turns out she was extremely wealthy, but no one would come out and talk to her. She informed the sales representative that she was moving out West with a relative and needed to get this place fixed up and sold. She thanked him for showing up and taking the time with her. Because the woman had no desire to write multiple checks, she wrote one check for the sum of $42,664. He made $7,400 in commission. One last piece to the story: The smart veteran sales rep turned the customer on to a Realtor who later sold the condo, and the Realtor gave the sales representative an $800 referral fee.

Question: Would you have stayed or left? Staying would have put $8,200 in your pocket.

DAY 14
In-home Sales Mantra No. 4:
Do You Believe in Yourself?

Look in the mirror and ask yourself: Would I buy my product from me? Would someone like or trust me? Will people respect me?

How do you feel about yourself? Do you feel in shape? Do you feel like you are on top of your sales game? Are you willing and able to learn from this book, or will you read it and throw it on the shelf because it was purchased for you? The choice is yours. But this is the best part: While you're sleeping, someone is selling and making money. While you're eating and playing, someone is achieving and moving forward. It starts with your inner self. Are you strong or weak?

You *must believe* you can. You can do everything in this book better than anyone else. If you doubt yourself, then it's time to look into another career. People enter and exit the In-home sales career daily.

Today we would like you to write down all the reasons you are going to succeed in this career. On a second sheet of paper write down the items you need to work on. Examples of areas that need improvement could be slowing down your speech when you present, better questioning techniques, better prospecting skills, or even prequalifying prospects. It could be your physical appearance, your grooming habits, or even the clothes you wear on the sales call. Only you know yourself, so make that list.

DAY 15
Mirror the Basics

On a very basic level your prospect is more comfortable with someone who is similar or like them versus someone who is dissimilar or unlike them. Think about your own preferences. If you are someone who talks rapidly and with passion about a topic, you are more comfortable when the person sitting across from you speaks with passion and at an accelerated rate. If you are someone who considers their words carefully and shows little emotion when discussing a topic, you will be suspicious if the person sitting across from you speaks rapidly and with passion. It's just the way we are. In the selling arena you should use this information to make your clients feel more comfortable with you. Once you recognize the prospect's rate of speech, tone, and level of emotion, you should adapt when you speak to him/her. This will make your prospect more comfortable with you and that will only benefit both parties. It's a win–win!

For today, identify your rate of speech, tone, and level of emotion. Practice doing the opposite of your style. Then look for someone who is unlike you and try to modify your approach. See how it feels. Keep track of how comfortable the customer appears to become by how long the conversation lasts and the amount of information he or she shares.

DAY 16
How You Identify the
Prospect's Behavioral Style

Now that you know your style, we want to look at how to identify the style of the person sitting across from you or the person
on the other end of the phone. Because you can't have prospects
take an assessment test, you have to identify their dominant style
from several observations. These observations can be made over
the phone or face to face. Clearly, being face to face will provide
much greater insight into their behavioral style, but you can pick
up many clues over the phone and even from their voice mail
messages.

There are two questions you must ask/observe, and these
become the basis for determining the customer's behavioral style.
The first observation is whether the person is an extrovert or an
introvert. Extroverts are outgoing, gregarious, enthusiastic, talkative, assertive, social, and active. Introverts are low key, deliberate, less emotional, quiet, shy, reserved, and contemplative.
Determining extrovert versus introvert is typically the easier of
the two observations you must make. Take a look at the list of
characteristics and think of your fellow workers, friends, and relatives. Can you separate the extroverts from the introverts?

The second observation you must make is whether the person
is task and detail oriented or whether they are people oriented.

Those who are task and detail oriented are busy, analytical, questioning, thoughtful, and organized. Those who are people oriented are friendly, cooperative, warm, agreeable, and sociable. This is typically the most difficult of the two observations you must make. Take a look at the list of characteristics and think of your fellow workers, friends, and relatives. Can you separate those who are task and detail oriented from those who are people oriented?

Now think about your prospects. Whether you are on the phone or face to face, you can hear or observe many of these traits. For today, make several phone calls to ice-cold prospects, particularly those who you never anticipate getting business from or even qualifying as an opportunity (translation: who cares what happens on these phone calls?). Listen to the way they talk. Listen to their voice mail greetings. How much detail do they leave in their greetings? How much emotion do you hear? When you get prospects on the phone, how much emotion do they show? How do they ask questions, and how much information do they want? Are they looking for a lot of detail? Do they sound optimistic or pessimistic? Are they pushy and impatient?

Next, when you are face to face, look for the following signs that will give you a good indication of whether they are introverted or extroverted, detail oriented or people oriented.

- Dominant: home and indications of their status in their home (prestigious committee/award plaques on wall), they initiate conversations, and are blunt/direct.

- Influencer: home with "experience" pictures (skiing, hiking, golfing, group/team), emotional, spontaneous, piles of mail (less organized), demonstrative (busy and animated gestures), optimistic.

D	C	Task/detail oriented
I	S	People oriented
Extrovert	Introvert	

- Steady: relaxed, cooperative, lots of family pictures, modest, patient.

- Compliant: quieter, questioning, perfectionist, distrustful, pessimistic.

Watch for these characteristics in others you meet on sales calls or hear over the phone. Begin to write down their behavioral styles wherever you keep information about your contacts so you can use the techniques you learn during the following days.

DAY 17
Ask Great Questions to Qualify

In your industry you need to ask specific questions to qualify your lead. For example:

- "How did you hear about us?"

- "What paper was that in?"

- "Where are you located?"

- "How soon are you planning to make a purchase?"

- "Once you decide to hire someone, when do you want to get the project started?"

- "Do you have the funds available or will you need assistance?"

- "Have you seen my product at another home? If yes, who? What did you like about it?"

- "Did they refer you to us?"

- "How long have you been thinking about getting this done?"

- "Did you get bids yet? How many do you plan on getting?"

- "Who is your insurance company/agent/telephone number?" (if this involves insurance)

If it's an outside project that requires a permit, you may ask, "Mr. Jones have you contacted your local permitting office yet?" This reinforces that you know your product and also gives you an indication of the prospect's sense of urgency.

Be careful not to prejudge your lead. For example, the prospect might say, "I am just shopping and plan to buy next year." Sometimes salespeople will go golfing and blow off the lead because they felt it was a not a good qualified lead. Just about the time they do this the next salesperson comes in behind you and makes a huge sale by raising the temperature of the lead by offering an incentive to buy now or by asking great questions to uncover the need to buy now versus next year. Prioritize your leads!

Pro Sales Tip: Never ask questions to which you should already know the answers. If you're in the kitchen business and your lead says that the prospect is interested in granite tops and solid cherry cabinets, don't call up and ask," Hi, Mr. Jones, Ron from XYZ Kitchens. I have a note on my desk and it says you're interested in a full kitchen install. What kind of cabinets and tops were you thinking of?" All this does is show that your company is not passing on the information and wasting the prospect's time. Instead, say, "Hi Mr. Jones, I have a note on my desk, and it says that your interested in a full kitchen restore. It also says you have an interest in granite tops and solid cherry wood cabinets, I can help in that area."

DAY 18
Send the Message Everyone
Is Buying from You

Customers want to buy from a company that is busy. Nothing sends the message that you have a great product better than the fact that other people are lining up to buy your product or service. The best way to send this message is to casually mention the other commitments you have.

When they begin to ask when you could come out to see them, make sure you don't say "any time!" as that reinforces no one is doing business with you. Instead say, "Mr. Jones, this is a pretty busy week coming up. Are you a morning or afternoon person?" This does two things: (1) You know when you want to call them or meet with them in the future (never call or meet with people when they are not at their best); and (2) they are selecting the appointment.

Use alternate choice questions to lead them to the appointment while continuing to reinforce that everyone is buying from you. Let's say they respond with "mornings are better." Simply pick another alternate such as "I can fit you in either Wednesday or Friday morning. Which do you prefer?" When the prospect says, "I will take the Friday slot," don't jump too soon. The rookie salesperson often responds eagerly with "Could I come see you, say Wednesday, then?" and the prospect responds with "No, just send me some information in the mail." Never ask a question that the prospect can respond with "no."

Get a real commitment and continue to reinforce that everyone is buying from you. This is not about being frantic or out of control. It is about finding a way to casually mention how busy you are with other installations, site visits, and sales appointments.

DAY 19
Dialing with Both Ears and a Smile

When you set the appointment and you hear the prospect say buzz words commonly used in your industry, chances are he or she has already talked to your competitor and learned the words from the previous sales representative. Listen closely on the phone.

Two key tips for that first phone contact:

1. *Remember this is your initial first impression with the prospect.* Have you ever spoken with someone over the phone and he/she made such a positive first impression that he/she stuck out like a tall person in the crowd? I recently purchased a new cell phone/PDA with all the bells and whistles. The first four times I called the company's customer service department it was an acceptable experience. But then I made another call and this call was special. Right from the start this person was different. The way she said hello suggested she was a nice person. She just gleamed. She acted like she was really concerned about my needs. I stayed on that call because I liked the person and the way she presented herself on the phone. If that person were in the **In-home** sales world, she could have made an appointment to sell me anything right then and there. The point is, she was pleasant, sincere, kind, interested, and professional.

2. *Always smile when talking on the phone.* Ever see movies that show successful phone salespeople such as good stockbrokers? Typically, they sell their products over the phone by making numerous phone calls. Next time you watch a movie like this take a close look at the dress code. They look great so they feel great, and that positive impression comes through over the phone. Simple as this is, if you look good, you feel good, and this projects right through the phone. Practice looking in the mirror while on the phone; visualize your own facial expressions. If you just got into an argument or some negative stimulus just occurred, hold off on setting this appointment until your mind is clear and positive.

Today practice setting appointments over the phone by calling yourself and leaving a message on your voicemail system. After you've left a few messages to yourself, listen to them and ask yourself the question: Would I agree to an appointment with that person?

DAY 20
In-home Sales Mantra No. 5: Don't Be Early, Don't Be Late, Be On Time

If you show up too early, you look like you are not busy and suggests no one is buying your product or service. If you show up late, you reinforce that there's a good possibility you will be late with your product or service and late with your follow-through. If you are 2 to 3 minutes early, then you are on time, and that equates to an **In-home** sales professional.

If you happen to arrive 5 to 15 minutes early, then park down the street and get yourself mentally prepared for the appointment.

Appointment Time Tips

Add additional time. It takes 25 percent more time to get wherever you are going than what you planned. If you know you need a solid hour, plan on one hour and 15 minutes.

Plan for bad weather. If you have an assigned territory, you should know most major roads, railroad tracks, and city traffic. As an **In-home** sales representative in the Chicago area my whole life, I really took pride in never being late for an appointment. The only challenge should be weather. So if there is any question, leave early, and you can use your idle time making phone calls or preparing for your appointments.

Call ahead if you have any chance of being late. With cell phones and GPS, there is very little reason you should be late. However, if you are going to be late make sure to call at least 5 minutes before the appointment and let the prospect know. He or she will respect that. Make sure you tell the prospect that being late is not your habit, but the traffic jam ahead of you was not in your travel plans.

DAY 21
In-home Sales Mantra No. 6:
Be positive or Be Quiet

You have heard it a million times: "If you can't say anything good, don't say anything at all." This is a life mantra that all sales professionals live by. This is what we teach our kids and the way we conduct ourselves in the workplace.

Negative people are magnets for other negative people, while positive people attract other positive people. Here are three thoughts to work through today.

1. Attempt to pair yourself with positive people today (and in the future). As you go about your life today, look for those people who are positive. Spend more time with them!

2. When you find yourself in a conversation with a negative person, simply change the subject (extinguish their negative thoughts) to something positive: the weather, a sports team, a positive story. If he or she doesn't continue with your positive discussion, then find a reason to move on.

3. Spend a few minutes writing all the positive things that have occurred or are occurring in your life. Reading this book is one of the positive items that should make the list. Our goal is to put you in a more positive mindset so by reading this book you are moving in a positive direction.

Start extinguishing every possible negative situation from here on forward and turn it into a positive. No matter what the situation is, make it positive.

DAY 22
Avoid Your Price and
Presentation on the Phone

Never ever give the price of your product over the phone. I can't count how many times I have trained or coached a new **In-home** sales representative and then heard him or her on the phone giving a price. They get so deep into product information that they feel obligated to go forward and provide pricing information too soon over the phone.

Understand two key points. First, all the prospect really wants is a price. Once you give it to him/her, the prospect is in control and you are out of control. What customer wants a multitude of salespeople coming through his or her home for two to three hours for each appointment? Second, if you can sell a product over the phone and get it signed with a down payment, why does your company even need you? Most companies have a policy against giving a price over the phone and there's a good reason for that policy. Until you get in front of the prospect and identify their needs and share how your product or service can address their needs, you have no business giving your price.

Be careful you don't start giving a sales presentation over the phone. The object of the qualifying phone call is to ask all the questions so you can determine how best to prepare for the actual **In-home** sales appointment. You should have your qualifying questions written down, in the order you typically ask them, to prevent yourself from going into a sales presentation. Oftentimes the prospect will actually draw you into your sales presentation over the phone by asking questions such as "tell me about your product/service." Be careful not to lay out all your features, benefits, and advantages right there on the qualifying call. This typically leaves nothing but the price to talk about, and why would they want you in their house just to talk about numbers? Ask the qualifying questions, and if they start asking other product/service-related questions, you intend to discuss on the appointment simply say, "That's a good question" or "I'm glad you asked that." Then say, "When we get together I will make sure I show you that product/service/feature/benefit/advantage as it's difficult to see without the information I cover when we meet."

Remember, the person who is asking the questions is in control. You want to be asking the questions and not talking about your product or service. If the prospect is asking all the questions, then this will lead into giving out a price. The key is that you need to get in front of them, sell yourself first, then your company story and product, and then the price. *Build the value.* Get their emotion level high.

Listed here are eight sample prequalifying questions that may work for your company when making an initial call. Remember you have two major tasks here: (1) prequalifying your lead and (2) setting an appointment.

1. How did you hear about us?

2. Where have you seen our product before? What did you like about it?

3. If you were referred to us, by whom?

4. What type of design do you have in mind for this project?

5. Once you decide to hire a deck company, when did you want the deck completed?

6. How many bids do you plan on getting? How many so far?

7. What budget do you have in mind? (if none) What is your "hope" number?

8. Have you talked to your local permitting authority yet?

DAY 23
Avoiding the Missing Decision Maker

When setting the appointment, make sure you get all the decision makers present. This is one of our favorite steps, as this is one of the most common challenges encountered by an **In-home** salesperson when trying to close a sale on the first call. No matter how great a sales rep you are or think you are, this is one *major* objection you cannot get past at the end of your initial sales appointment when asking the prospects to buy. It's called the one-leg appointment. It simply means the customer can't make a decision without asking his or her spouse, significant other, son or daughter, parent or another person who is needed when making purchasing decisions. Could you make a $35,000–$65,000 kitchen decision without involving someone else, such as your spouse or significant other? Companies that set up appointments for their **In-home** sales representatives must address this with their call centers or whoever takes the incoming calls and/or sets appointments.

In today's world you cannot just ask if the spouse will be present. This is rude and could be offensive. You must identify all the parties involved in making the decision, but you cannot alienate the person you are talking to by implying he or she must not be able to make the decision alone. This is a very narrow line, and one we spend a great deal of time on with our clients during coaching and training.

Here is the general script for reducing one-leg appointments. After you have asked most, if not all, of your qualification questions ask: "Mr. Jones, at (your company name) we have a lot of options—color, handles and pulls, design, and the final layout. Who, other than yourself, will be assisting you in deciding on the color, handles and pull, design and final layout?"

The concept is to tell them that there are so many decisions to make that if anyone else is involved, they really should be there. Giving the prospect options that are complex improves this process. Options that sound difficult will increase the probability that the prospect will want help making a decision and will tell you who else is involved with the decision.

If the prospect responds, "Well, yes, my wife Peggy helps out," then ask, "Great, will Peggy be able to join us on Friday morning?" If the prospect says "yes," then you're in good shape. If the prospect responds with a "no, she is working that morning," then we recommend you say, "What is a better day or time to get together so Peggy is there?"

Along the way you may get resistance to this process. They might say they can handle the appointment themselves or that their spouses/significant others/other decision-making parties told them to "just get it handled." This is a smokescreen; never buy into it. It's important that they know your schedule is tight and that both are there to see your presentation. Remember you're in control until you give them control.

DAY 24
Preparing for the Call
with the Driver

We believe you can improve your sales results by identifying the prospect's behavioral style and the way he or she makes buying decisions and then modify your approach at four points in the sales process:

1. Pre-call preparation

2. Appointment/call itself

3. Closing

4. Follow- up

Today we will cover how to prepare for a sales call for one of the four styles: Dominant/drivers. In the next few days we will cover the other three styles: Influencers, Compliants, and the Steady. While many of the ideas we share today may already be part of your pre-call sales strategy, we recommend aligning the steps with the customer's behavioral style.

Here is how to prepare for a call with a prospect you have identified as having a Dominant behavioral style:

- Show what's in it for them. Because customers with a Dominant behavioral style are bottom-line oriented, you need to lay out the benefit(s) they will receive with your product/

service early in the discussion. Be prepared to show how your product/service is a good investment and be prepared to get there fast.

- Develop a list of "best in class" references. Identify several "best in class" references that have used your product/service so you can share the list with them. Drivers like to be associated with other "best in class" customers.

- Thicken your skin. Drivers tend to be direct, blunt, and outspoken, which may erode your self-confidence. Go into the appointment with strong self-confidence.

- Stroke their egos. Drivers have a strong ego drive, and it would benefit you if you could share information that would reinforce their accomplishments. Do your homework and figure out where you could introduce these reinforcements into the sales call.

- They like to "own" the solution. Drivers like to put their mark on decisions. Look for ways to tie their ideas to your presentation.

- Have your facts. Because Drivers have strong egos, you should avoid disagreeing with them and instead focus on the facts. The key is to come prepared with the facts or you run the risk of disagreeing with them on a personal level.

- Develop an agenda. Drivers like structure and are typically very busy. Bringing an agenda to the appointment gives them confidence you are not going to get off track.

DAY 25
Preparing for the Call
with the Influencer

Here is how to prepare for a call with a prospect you have identified as having an Influencer behavioral style:

- Summarize your key points. Influencers tend to get off track and get you off track. As a result you need to summarize your key points that go with your demonstration.

- Load up on the visuals. Influencers like to "experience" what they are buying, and something that is visual has the greatest connection; use pictures, graphs, samples, and so forth. Note: If your product/service is something that can be left with the prospects so they can try it out, this is another great way to connect with them.

- Develop "cutting-edge" references for your product/service. Influencers love to be with the "in crowd," so sharing specific examples of who has used your product/service from that crowd will have a very positive impact.

- Bring a compelling offer/promotion. If you have any special promotions or offers to act as an incentive, this is important for Influencers, who tend to be spontaneous. This compelling offer may just be the incentive they need to move forward.

- Remember the personal side. Think of some personal prompts you may want to use during your first conversation: cars, boats, sports, gardening, horses, pets, and so forth. Influencers like to socialize.

For today take a look at the appointments you have with Influencers and review the list. Prepare accordingly and you'll have more confidence going into the sale.

DAY 26
Preparing for the Call
with the Compliant

Here is how to prepare for a call with a prospect you have identified as having a Compliant behavioral style:

- Have all the information. Compliants ask a lot of questions and will become suspicious if you do not have the answers. It's best to be overprepared versus underprepared with a Compliant. This information might include:

  – Pros and cons of each option you are offering

  – Financial parameters and justification for each option

  – Any reputable third-party industry information about the options.

- Be honest. If you have a situation that has not worked with your product and the prospect may know about it, be prepared with an answer, should it come up.

- Develop a list of credible references. The key word is credible. If there's anyone who will actually follow up on your references it will be the Compliant. Also, if you have a credible reference that would be willing to speak with the Compliant, compile that information before the call. (It is best if the reference also has a Compliant behavioral style.)

- Bring brochures. If you have brochures that have additional data, this may be helpful to dispel their suspicions or help you answer questions. Oftentimes the Compliant will ask a question the salesperson cannot answer, and then the Compliant will find the answer for the salesperson in the brochure.

- Develop a step-by-step approach. Make sure your presentation covers all the information you believe they would ever need.

- Develop an agenda. Compliants like structure, and bringing an agenda to the appointment gives them confidence you are not going to get off track.

As you can tell from the length of the list, calling on Compliants requires additional preparation. Build this into your schedule if you typically call on prospects with a Compliant behavioral style.

DAY 27
In-home Sales Mantra No. 7:
Be Polite and Find a Connection

Never start an **In-home** sales appointment by asking if you can use their bathroom. These people just met you; do you think they want a stranger in their home playing around with their toilet and looking in the cabinets? Use the gas station down the street and plan your time accordingly.

Look around the home and see if you notice anything that could connect you and the prospects together. For example, maybe they were in the service and so were you. Maybe they are fans of the same sports team that you support. As you engage in this rapport-building conversation, make sure you let them talk. People love to talk about themselves and their interests.

We have seen new **In-home** sales representatives walk into a house and brag about themselves, something they own, someone they know, or even how great their kids are, as if they are trying to beat the prospect's story. Do you think these prospects care about you? They just met you and may never see you again. If you spend their time talking about you, they will never want to see you again!

This is the warm-up stage. Bonding here is vital. Remember, people buy from people they like.

DAY 28
In-home Sales Mantra No. 8:
All Scales Up

When you're new to the sales career, your enthusiasm is at its highest peak and your product knowledge is at its lowest. The key is get them both up and keep them both up.

Shortly after you leave any training session or seminar, you're typically pumped up and your emotion and enthusiasm are very high. The chance of you running a lead and making a sale at this point is very good. After three to six months your product knowledge will grow, but your enthusiasm may decrease as you experience rejection and the excitement of your new career wears off. The ultimate goal is to keep both your desire for product knowledge and your enthusiasm scaling up. Here are some key points in keeping all the scales up:

- Have your home and family life in order.

- Make sure your finances are in order and get out of debt.

- Keep your health and weight in check.

- Always stay on top of your product industry and know your competition.

- Always continue your sales education on a daily/weekly basis.

- Reward yourself for a great month in sales.

- Always have attainable goals in place. Reward yourself for hitting a short-term goal.

When you are on top of your game, your peers may get jealous of your success. They may even try to bring you down. Other times you will simply find yourself in the middle of a negative discussion about your company, your trading area, or your product and service. Don't participate in these discussions. Excuse yourself and get back to business. If you do this, it will be all scales up with earning, learning, and energy.

DAY 29
Preparing for the Call
with the Steady

Here is how to prepare for a call with a prospect you have identified as having a Steady behavioral style:

- Remember the personal side. Review your notes of personal discussions you've had in the past with this customer. Or, if this is the first appointment, think of some personal prompts you may want to use during your first conversation. Those with a Steady behavioral style like people and enjoy a light personal conversation.

- Go light with the details. Have top-line information prepared for your presentation, such as a headline in a newspaper, because the Steady style is not much into the details. Have the backup information ready in case they have additional questions.

- Show me! Develop evidence of how your product/service has worked and also other solutions on the market that have not worked. The Steady wants to make sure he or she is not the first to try your product/service.

- Develop a list of credible references. If you have a credible reference that would be willing to speak with the Steady, compile that information before the call. (It is best if the reference also has a Steady behavioral style.)

- Be honest. If you have a situation that has not worked with your product and the prospect may know about it, be prepared with an answer, should it come up.

- Bring a compelling offer/promotion along. If you have any special promotions or offers that act as an incentive make sure to share it with your prospect.

For today, take a look at the appointments (phone or face to face) you have with a customer who has a Steady behavioral style and review the list. Prepare accordingly and you'll have more confidence going into the sale.

DAY 30
Step 3: Meet and Greet—
on Time and on Target

In this career you have to love kids and animals. It's almost a guarantee that when you drive up to the home and meet the 150-pound dog it is going to jump all over your nice clean clothes. Most people's pets are like their kids so you have to be careful to make a positive first impression with the pets as well as with the prospects. Make sure you take the time to show affection for their animal. Bringing treats for pets is another great idea but make sure you ask the owners if you can give the pet the treat. There's nothing worse than giving a treat only to find out the pet has a digestive disorder. Although, if you are in the carpet cleaning business, this may be a great way to get the prospects' attention.

As you drive into the driveway, if the pet approaches and you are concerned about it ripping you apart, the best technique is to stay in the car and appear as if you are trying to locate something from your briefcase. Root around the car, lean over the backseat, and make it appear you are looking for something versus just being afraid of the animal. The owner will typically come out, call off "killer," and you are back in business. Also it's a good idea to have a clean vehicle inside and out, since the job site could be down the road and the prospect asks you for a lift.

This is a good time to discuss your cell phone. If you decide to bring it in the home, make sure you put in on vibrate or better yet, completely turn it off. It's very annoying to take notes or execute a professional presentation with your phone ringing off the hook. You may even leave it in your vehicle but we find the phone will come in handy if you need to make a call for a higher authority close (see Appendix A-2).

Finally, upon your arrival observe what kind of cars they drive, kids toys and any other observations that could help you make a connection with the prospects.

DAY 31
The First Impression

Only bring a brochure and your business card with you to the door. Do not bring your complete demo case as this will scare them and they might not even let you in the door. I like to leave all my demo samples in the car. If you have an outside product such as decks, fencing, siding, paint, landscaping, windows, gutters, roofing, and room additions, you will need to go back outside and inspect the site. Even if you sell kitchens or baths, you should still go in with a business card and brochure and, after you get a good feeling about the opportunity, you can go out and get your presentation book and samples.

It's best to park in the street rather than in their driveway. There's nothing that breaks the flow of the sale than if you have to go back outside and move your car because it is blocking someone in the driveway.

Upon your arrival, go up to the door and knock or ring the doorbell and step back at least 3 to 4 feet. If they don't answer right away, do not walk up and look into the glass door or any windows. Continue to knock/ring and step back until they answer. The key is you want to be back from the door 3 to 4 feet when they open the door so you won't have to step back and break eye contact.

When they invite you in it's vital to ask if it's necessary to remove your shoes. You must understand that this is their first impression of you. If you smoke, it's essential to use a smoke odor eliminator. There are many sprays you can use on your clothes and gum/breath mints that will eliminate smoke odor. Remember, you are the invited guest in their home. The first 15 to 45 seconds you're getting sized up. Now for another golden rule:

Pro Sales Tip:: Do *not* talk about religion or politics, ever. If they support one political party and you support the other, do you think arguing about this will move you closer to the sale?

This is a good time to look around and make sure all the decision makers are present or will be present upon your arrival. Look for parked cars upon your arrival, for shoes and pictures. If you sensed that this person was single, yet you see pictures around the home of the prospect and another person, you might have gotten misled in Step 1 (the lead). Be careful, as you can't always be sure and you don't want to jump to an incorrect conclusion that causes you to change your demeanor and make them uncomfortable. Stay in form and in time, by bonding and connecting, you will find out the situation.

How long should I spend on building rapport? I am routinely asked this question in training seminars and the answer is simple. You will get a feel from the prospects when they are ready to talk about your product or service. Develop your instincts around knowing when it's time to move to the next step. Some sales representatives are pros at warming up prospects and some are so stiff you wonder if they are breathing.

Timing is vital. Make sure you stay off the product or service discussion and let them talk about themselves.

DAY 32
Adapting to the Dominant/Driver at the Appointment

People buy from people they like. This is not news to anyone. Prospects are more comfortable buying from a sales professional they like and are more comfortable and willing to purchase from a salesperson similar to themselves. While similarities in age, background, nationality, lifestyle, and even dress are shown to create a positive response, our focus is on behavioral similarities.

If you recall back on Day 15 we discussed the importance of modifying your approach and mirror, in a very subtle way, the style of your prospect. Rate and volume of speech are two obvious examples. We now want to take this concept a step further and discuss *specific* ways in which you need to adapt during the sales call, whether on the phone or face to face, depending on the behavioral style of the prospect. The type of adaptation you make will also depend on your style. Take your behavioral style(s) from Days 8 and 9. Today we will cover the adaptations you should consider making when you identify your prospect as a Dominant/Driver behavioral style (from Day 16).

If your behavioral style is also a Dominant/Driver, then consider adapting in the following manner:

- Present your information in a linear, organized manner. Go step by step and be prepared to speed up as they direct.

- Be direct. Get to the point quickly, as they are typically impatient.

- Move fast, as they are comfortable deciding quickly.

- Offer alternatives during the conversation. Allow them to decide between options, as they want to make the decision.

- Give them recognition. Use "you said/wanted/asked " types of comments to reinforce their ego.

- Look for opportunities to let them win. They enjoy a challenge and winning is important. Make sure that you also achieve your goals.

- Disagree with the facts, not the person. It's OK to stand firm, however, disagree about the facts and do not disagree with them on a personal level.

- Don't dictate to them, as being in control makes them more comfortable with you.

- You also like a challenge, so enjoy the combat. They expect you to hold your ground.

- It's a two-way street. Don't let them overpower you.

If your behavioral style is Influencer/Expressive, then consider adapting to the Dominant/Driver in the following manner:

- Avoid physical contact. Actions such as putting your hands on the customer's back and touching his or her arm are off limits. Drivers like their space and this includes their personal space (attention close talkers).

- Do not joke. Your natural desire to create levity will be unappreciated.

- Be direct. Get to the point quickly, as Drivers are typically impatient.

- Avoid getting off-track. Present your information in a linear, organized manner. Go step by step and be prepared to speed up as they direct.

- "Stay in form" with your presentation. Don't become too personal in the discussion. Follow their lead relative to any personal discussion.

- Look for opportunities to let them win. They enjoy a challenge and winning is important. Make sure that you also achieve your goals.

- Give them recognition. Use "you said/wanted/asked" types of comments to reinforce their ego.

- Avoid ambiguity or uncertainty. Drivers reward knowledge and confidence.

- Take copious notes. This reinforces that what they are saying is important.

- Do not over-promise. Your natural desire to please the prospect may cause you to over-commit. Avoid this trap at all cost.

- Close confidently. Your natural desire to avoid confrontation may deter you from moving the sale forward. Ask for their business.

- Don't let them overpower you. You have a goal so don't allow them to overpower you.

If your behavioral style is Steady/Amiable, then consider adapting to the Dominant/Driver in the following manner:

- Strengthen your resolve. Mirror the strength of the Driver since he or she will typically be strong. It's OK to remain friendly but stay strong.

- Take copious notes. This reinforces that what they are saying is important.

- Be confident! Don't let them intimidate you. You have a goal so don't allow them to intimidate you.

- Present your information in a linear, organized manner. Go step by step and be prepared to speed up as they direct.

- Speed it up. You must proceed faster than you feel comfortable during the appointment. Drivers move fast.

- Give them recognition. Use "you said/wanted/asked" types of comments to reinforce their ego.

- Look for opportunities to let them win. They enjoy a challenge and winning is important.

- Avoid ambiguity or uncertainty. Drivers reward knowledge and confidence.

- Disagree with the facts, not the person. Stay focused on the facts and details when not in agreement with the Driver.

- Close sooner! Your natural desire to avoid confrontation may deter you from moving the sale forward. The Driver appreciates the value of wrapping up the sale so ask for the order.

- Don't let them overpower you. You have a goal and you must achieve that goal.

If your behavioral style is Compliant/Analytical, then consider adapting to the Dominant/Driver in the following manner:

- Be brief and to the point. Get to the point quickly, as they are typically impatient and direct.

- Touch upon the high points. The Driver is interested in the bottom line.

- Do not overuse data. Your natural tendency is to cover all the data. Only share the additional data if the Driver requests it.

- Speed it up. You must proceed faster than you feel comfortable during the appointment. Drivers move fast!

- Give them recognition. Use "you said/wanted/asked" types of comments to reinforce their egos.

- Satisfy their strong egos. Look for opportunities to reinforce them and their accomplishments.

- Look for opportunities to let them win. They enjoy a challenge and winning is important, but make sure you also achieve your goals.

Put this information into a format where you can easily access it as you prepare your appointment strategy with a prospect/customer.

DAY 33
Adapting to the Influencer/ Expressive at the Appointment

Today we will cover the adaptations you should consider making when you identify your prospect has a Influencer/Expressive behavioral style (from Day 16).

If your behavioral style is Dominant/Driver, then consider adapting to the Influencer/expressive in the following manner:

- Be personal and friendly. Warm up the appointment with a sincere conversation about something personal.

- Don't be in a hurry, take your time. The appointment may not stay on track so don't appear in a hurry as that will make the buyer uncomfortable.

- Joke around, have some fun. Follow their lead.

- Allow them to talk. They love to talk so don't dominate.

- Provide recognition. They enjoy being reinforced so look for an opportunity to provide recognition.

- Don't talk down to them. Your natural tendency to lead the conversation may be interpreted as talking down to them. Be careful!

- Talk about people. They enjoy talking about others and their experiences, so look for opportunities to leverage similar contacts and interests.

- Prepare for a lot of spontaneity. The conversation may appear to be unstructured with spontaneous thoughts and off-the-track discussions. Allow them the flexibility to get off track and they will be more comfortable with you.

- Keep the presentation at a high level. Don't get mired in details, as they will lose interest.

- Share ways to minimize risk and get them into the product/ service sooner. As they see the risk go down, they will move forward.

If your behavioral style is also Influencer/Expressive, then consider adapting to the Influencer/Expressive in the following manner:

- Be yourself. Have fun on the appointment and generate energy from their stories.

- Let them talk more than you. They should be doing most of the talking, as they are more comfortable when they are talking.

- Listen to their stories. They enjoy sharing stories so don't interrupt or attempt to "one-up" them.

- Look for opportunities to give them recognition during your presentation.

- Look for opportunities to weave in your product/service presentation. Be careful not to waste too much time talking about your product/service. They will view this as "business" and may be uncomfortable.

- Make sure you achieve your goal. Your tendency to enjoy the conversation must be balanced with your need to reach your goal.

If your behavioral style is Steady/Amiable then consider adapting to the Influencer/Expressive in the following manner:

- Keep the details to a minimum as you share with them the benefits of your product/service.

- Listen to their stories. They enjoy sharing stories so sit back and enjoy the conversation.

- Have fun with them. Enjoy the discussion!

- Allow them to talk but make sure you keep the appointment on track.

- Look for opportunities to give them recognition during your presentation.

- Share ways to minimize risk and get them into the product/service sooner. Make it easy for them to accept your product/service.

- Share key dates and problems. Provide them with any time-sensitive deadlines and confirm throughout the appointment the problems that surface. Use these deadlines to move the sale forward.

- Make sure you achieve your goal. Keep a clear line of sight to your goal during the appointment as their lack of focus may distract you.

If your behavioral style is Compliant/Analytical, then consider adapting to the Influencer/Expressive in the following manner:

- Keep the presentation at a high level. Don't get mired in details as they will lose interest.

- Use top-line information whenever possible. Minimize your natural approach of covering all the details by offering summary information.

- Prepare for a lot of spontaneity. The conversation may appear to be unstructured with spontaneous thoughts and off-the-track discussions. Allow them the flexibility to wander.

- Be friendly and fun. Leave your detail focus behind.

- Ask more questions. Instead of stating information, turn it around. Look for opportunities to link their answers to your goal.

- Allow them to talk but make sure you keep the appointment on track. Let them do most of the talking but steer the conversation toward your goal.

- Share ways to minimize risk and get them into the product/service sooner. Make it easy for them by reducing their risk.

Put this information into a format where you can easily access it as you prepare your appointment strategy with a prospect/customer.

DAY 34
In-home Sales Mantra No. 9:
Not All Prospects Look the Same

Prepare for everything and anything when you knock on the door. Your first task is getting the prospect to like you. Top sales closers have mastered this art, and so will you after you have completed this book. If you ever watch other people while in line at the ballpark or while sitting in the mall, you know that there are very different types of people in this world. Not only do people look different but they also act in different ways.

When you knock on the door, you don't know what might have happened in the minutes or hours prior to your arrival. They may not be in a good mood or they may have just won the lottery. There are many different economic situations you will encounter. We have poor, wealthy, and the "get me dones." The "get me dones" are people that will buy anything if you can get them financed. These are typically easy to close the sale, but 95 percent of the time you cannot get financing for the "get me dones."

Occasionally you will knock on the door and the prospect is just like you. The key is to make sure you adapt to be just like your customer. When you knock on that door, it's vital that you are prepared to adapt. This is a huge part of your selling process. If you adapt and stay in control of the selling cycle, then you will overcome every obstacle on the way to that sale.

For today just look around and notice the different types of people in the world. Get ready to adapt to every single one of them because that's the life of an **In-home** sales professional.

DAY 35
In-home Sales Mantra No. 10:
One Hour Per Day Times
Three Years Makes You an Expert

Study your craft and in no time you will be an expert in your product or service area. In today's world, there is no shortage of sales knowledge. Given the fact that you are probably spending a fair amount of time in your vehicle, we recommend you spend at least 60 minutes per day reading a book on sales or listening to audiobooks.

Most **In-home** sales representatives drive to their leads. Why not plug in a CD of a sales trainer? As a rule of thumb you will need to listen to the CD six times before you master the information. We recommend listening about three times and then listening while taking notes. Pick up a basic sales training book or audiobook once a year, because going back to the basics on an annual basis is the best practice for the **In-home** sales professional. Every top sports professional practices daily and goes back to the basics once a year.

It also helps to find a few of your favorite segments in a book or on a CD that really gives you confidence and listen/review this 10 to 15 minutes before the appointment. Go down the street and plug in that CD or get a section out of a book and get geared up for the appointment.

For today, go to the local bookstore, library, or www.salesoc-tane.com (click the In-home sales tab) and pick up a selection of audiobooks, motivational CDs, or books on sales.

DAY 36
Adapting to the Steady/Amiable at the Appointment

Today we will cover the adaptations you should consider making when you identify your prospect as a Steady/Amiable behavioral style (from Day 16).

If your behavioral style is Dominant/Driver, then consider adapting to the Steady/Amiable in the following manner:

- Don't control or dominate. Methodically go through your presentation and allow them to decide how fast they wish to proceed.

- Begin with your personal connections to build rapport.

- Show sincerity. Be honest and sincere during your presentation, as they are very good at sizing up character.

- Start with the problem/issue and move slowly through each option and confirm there are no questions following each one: "Does that make sense?" or "Did I cover that OK?"

- Listen carefully. Pay attention to the conversation and don't appear to lose interest, which makes them less comfortable with you.

- Slow down and relax. Your natural approach is to move directly and quickly through the agenda. This will make them very uncomfortable.

- Build trust. The Steady is typically suspicious, and you must bring them to a point where they trust you.

- Give them the facts they need. Don't go too deep with information; stay on a higher level with less detail.

- Tie everything you can back to what they currently use or are comfortable using. They do not like to change, so link your product/service to their comfort level.

- Get "little" agreements along the way. Ask confirmation questions such as "Is this what you're looking for?" or "Does this look like it will work?" They are very loyal buyers so getting them to agree along the way begins to obligate them.

- Do not push. Take your time. They will not proceed fast. However, because they are loyal buyers, the longer sales cycle is worth the investment in time.

If your behavioral style is Influencer/Expressive, then consider adapting to the Steady/Amiable in the following manner:

- Be friendly and personal and earn their trust. Lower your energy level a bit and use your natural personality to build a friendly, personal environment.

- Let them talk while you ask questions. Your natural tendency is to share information rapidly. In this case you want to ask more questions and let them talk.

- Slow down and relax. Your natural approach is to talk fast and have a lot of energy. This will make them very uncomfortable.

- Start with the problem/issue and move slowly through each option and confirm there are no questions following each one: "Does that make sense?" or "Did I cover that OK?"

- Give them the facts. Don't "wing it" with details. Share factual information that you can stand behind.

- Provide assurances of your promises. Share references or guarantees to minimize their risk. If this is a change from their current situation, these assurances are essential.

- Get "little" agreements along the way. Ask confirmation questions such as "Is this what you're looking for?" or "Does this look like it will work?" They are very loyal buyers, so getting them to agree along the way will begin to obligate them.

- Tie your solution back to what they currently use or are comfortable using. Whereas you may like change and to make spontaneous decisions, they do not, so link your product/service to their comfort level.

- Do not push. Take your time. They will not proceed fast. However, because they are loyal buyers, the longer sales cycle is worth the investment in time.

If your behavioral style is also Steady/Amiable, then consider adapting to the Steady/Amiable in the following manner:

- Be yourself. Move through the appointment in a very relaxed and comfortable manner and lean toward a friendly discussion.

- Provide assurances of your promises. Share references or guarantees to minimize their risk. If this is a change from their current situation, these assurances are essential.

- Be factual. Give them the facts of your product/service but don't go too deep with information; stay on a higher level with less detail.

- When they agree with a particular point you should assure them they are headed in the right direction.

- Expand your "team." Introduce them to or mention your managers, service managers, inside customer support staff, and other team members to increase their confidence with your team.

- Tie everything you can back to what they currently use or are comfortable using. Identify the ease of going with your product/service.

- Keep sight of your goal. Make sure you accomplish your goal.

If your behavioral style is Compliant/Analytical, then consider adapting to the Steady/Amiable in the following manner:

- Begin the appointment with something personal. Avoid launching into the details of the appointment too quickly.

- Move slowly. Set aside ample time for the appointment, as it will move more slowly than sales calls with other behavioral styles.

- Provide facts and figures but keep the conversation at a higher level. You can go into greater detail if they ask for more detailed information.

- Do not overcontrol or push. Your natural tendency to control the details and push through the extensive information you brought may cause the buyer to disengage from the conversation.

- Develop trust by providing assurances. Share credible references and guarantees that will build their trust in your product/service.

- Tie everything you can back to what they currently use or are comfortable using. Identify the ease of going with your product/service.

- Focus on reliability and service. Share information regarding the reliability of your product and service in order to satisfy their risk-averse nature.

Put this information into a format where you can easily access it as you prepare your appointment strategy with a prospect/customer.

DAY 37
Adapting to the Compliant/Analytical at the Appointment

Today we will cover the adaptations you should consider making when you identify your prospect has a Compliant/Analytical behavioral style (from Day 16)

If your behavioral style is Dominant/Driver, then consider adapting to the Compliant/Analytical in the following manner:

- Be patient and slow. Don't allow your Driver nature to make them uncomfortable.

- Give them data. Make sure you bring all the detailed information that supports your presentation.

- Use brochures with data. The more material you can share with them, the more credible your case.

- Give more information than you'd like. Go above and beyond what you would normally expect a customer would need to make a decision.

- Start with the issue and move slowly through each option and confirm there are no questions following each one: "Does that make sense?" or "Did I cover that OK?" Be detailed.

- Give them credit. Reinforce them sincerely and honestly throughout the appointment by giving them credit for their questions and/or concerns that support your product/service.

- Keep control. Your driven nature may cause you to get frustrated with their cautious approach, so be aware of your persistence.

- Keep it all business. Do not talk personally unless they initiate a personal discussion. Even then, keep it to a minimum and get back to business.

- Do not push. They make thoughtful, careful decisions and will become suspicious if you continue to push them toward a close.

- There will be many questions coming your way, so don't get defensive. If you don't have the answer, identify how you will get the information and confirm they are comfortable with your plan/timeframe.

- Stress the "reality" of the risk associated with not moving forward (if they consistently show an inability to move forward). Be careful not to raise "unrealistic" risks or you will lose credibility fast.

If your behavioral style is Influencer/Expressive, then consider adapting to the Compliant/Analytical in the following manner:

- Keep your distance. Respect their space and do not touch if you are on a face-to-face appointment.

- Do not be too personal. Cordial is one thing, but your natural social style will make them suspicious. Keep it friendly but direct.

- Give them the facts, figures, and proof. Give them more details than you would be comfortable receiving if you were in the buyer's position. They want details so give it to them.

- Do not waste time. They will want to stick to business so respect their desire and stick to the agenda.

- There will be many questions coming your way so don't get defensive. If you don't have the answer, identify how you will get the information and confirm they are comfortable with your plan/timeframe.

- Start with the issue and move slowly through each option and confirm there are no questions following each one: "Does that make sense?" or "Did I cover that OK?" Be detailed.

- Answer all their questions. Don't dismiss any of their questions. If they ask it, then you must answer it.

- Reference the source of any information you share that is not your own. Your credibility is one of the pieces to the puzzle of connecting with this style. Make sure you share the sources of your information in an effort to gain credibility.

- Be concerned with details. Take an interest in their detail orientation. Even if you don't feel it is important to the decision, if they are interested, you need to be interested.

- Confirm you have given them what they want along the way. Continually check in with questions such as "Is that what you were looking for?" or "Is there anything else you need on that point?"

- Occasionally reinforce them sincerely and honestly by giving them credit for their questions and/or concerns. Being accurate is important to them so reinforce that characteristic.

- Stress the "reality" of the risk associated with not moving forward (if they consistently show an inability to move forward). Be careful not to raise "unrealistic" risks or you will lose credibility fast.

If your behavioral style is Steady/Amiable, then consider adapting to the Compliant/Analytical in the following manner:

- Keep your distance. Respect their space and do not touch if you are on a face-to-face appointment.

- Do not be too personal. It's OK to be friendly and cordial but avoid trying to be their friend. Instead be direct and follow their lead regarding personal discussion.

- Do not fear their skeptical nature. Do not take their skepticism as a lack of confidence in your sales ability. This is their nature, so recognize their constant questioning as a desire to make a correct decision.

- Start with the issue and move slowly through each option and confirm there are no questions following each one: "Does that make sense?" or "Did I cover that OK?" Be detailed.

- Follow through on details. Go deeper in the details than you would normally do if you were making a similar decision.

- Occasionally reinforce them by giving them credit for their questions and/or concerns. They pride themselves on making good observations so reinforce this characteristic.

- Answer all questions with facts. Avoid offering your insight or personal input and stay focused on the facts. Their decision will be made with factual information, so give them everything you have in your bag.

- Reference the source of any information you share that is not your own. Credibility is an essential characteristic to help them become more comfortable with you and your product or service, so provide your credible source(s) of information.

- Stress the "reality" of the risk associated with not moving forward (if they consistently show an inability to move forward). Be careful not to raise "unrealistic" risks or you will lose credibility fast.

If your behavioral style is also Compliant/Analytical, then consider adapting to the Compliant/Analytical in the following manner:

- Be yourself. Your natural tendency to stay focused on the task at hand will connect with the buyer(s) and make them comfortable with your approach.

- Give them the data they request. Provide them with the detailed answers they are looking for even if you would do it differently.

- Examine pros and cons. You will naturally evaluate your own product or service before you proceed with selling it to a prospective buyer. Share the pros and cons you used with your evaluation as this will make them confident in your analytical abilities.

- Remain in control. Your natural desire to be accurate may cause you to engage should the buyer choose a different path. Allow the buyer(s) to choose their own path.

- Provide credible references and evidence to support your claims.

- Stay focused on your goal. Your natural approach is to focus more on the process of making the decision and less on the outcome. As a sales professional, you must balance your desire to help the buyer make a correct decision with the need to meet your goal of a sale. Don't lose sight of that goal.

Put this information into a format where you can easily access it as you prepare your appointment strategy with a prospect/customer.

DAY 38
Manage Your Expectations

Confidence is a major contributor to sales success. All other issues being equal, the In-home sales professional with confidence will outperform the salesperson who lacks confidence.

One of the ways to improve your confidence is by managing your expectations based on your fit with the style of your prospect or customer. Some styles are complementary in the sales process and others are not. Once you finish today's material you will no doubt recall a time when you struggled with a prospect or customer. When you look at the chart you may find that his/her style was either a poor or fair match with your style. Those situations often erode our self-confidence and have a negative impact on subsequent sales calls.

By managing our expectations going into the sales situation we can keep our self-confidence intact. The process works like this. First, locate your dominant style as the salesperson on the chart. Next, identify the style of your customer along the top of the chart below using the techniques we discussed on Day 16.

Let's say you are an Influencer, like me. (If you have a blend of more than one, you can take your other dominant styles into consideration.) Based on the chart, if I am selling to another Influencer, I have a *good* match and there's a *good* chance of a successful call. If I am selling to a Driver, I also have a good chance. But, when it comes to the Steady, I only have a *fair* chance, and with the Compliant I have a *poor* chance. This is very important for me to know. When I find myself in a selling situation where the customer has a Compliant style I need to recognize that I will have to adapt my natural style and approach in a number of ways.

Those "adaptations" may feel very unnatural or against my normal approach to selling and typically does not feel as good as when I am selling to a Driver or Influencer. By recognizing this fact I can manage my expectations for the call and not allow it to substantially impact my self-confidence.

For today, recall several recent sales calls that have gone well and several sales calls that were a challenge. Try to remember each customer and identify his or her behavioral style from Day 16. Using the chart, see how often the calls that have gone well were because you had a good or excellent match with the customer and how often the calls that were a challenge were because the customer was either a *poor* or *fair* match. By managing your expectations you will maintain your self-confidence, which is critical to a sales professional.

		Customer			
S **A** **L** **E** **S** **P** **E** **R** **S** **O** **N**	Style	Driver	Influencer	Steady	Compliant
	Driver	Good	Good	Fair	Poor
	Influencer	Good	Good	Fair	Poor
	Steady	Fair	Good	Excellent	Excellent
	Compliant	Poor	Poor	Excellent	Excellent

DAY 39
Disarming Statement

The disarming statement sets an expectation for both the buyer and the seller. It's important to get prospects comfortable that you are not going to pressure them into a sale. The best way to disarm the customer is to address the issue right before you get your presentation book and samples. Or, if you are doing an outside walk-around, you can use the disarming statement at that time. Here is an example of a disarming statement: "Mr. Jones, I am going out to get some samples for you. At any time if you don't like my colors or samples, I can pack my goods and be on my way. I can take a 'no' just the same as a 'yes,' fair enough?"

This statement is designed to let prospects know that if you or your product/service does not fit their needs, you will be on your way out of there. On the other hand, it's a way of saying, "I might ask you to buy later if you like what you see." People respect the statement because, if they really truly do not like your samples or product, why waste your time and theirs?

If you work for a superior company, your price is most likely mid to high range. If this is the case, then you also need to add these words, "Also, Mr. Jones, we most likely will not be the cheapest guy on the block, but in a minute I will explain why." This is the time to start observing which behavioral style your prospect might be. Knowing this in advance will give you a major edge so you can adjust your style to ultimately make the sale.

DAY 40
Step 4: Visual Inspection, Part 1

With most **In-home** sales situations, you are selling a product or service that affects a physical area. In some cases you may need specific information regarding the physical space in order to complete your design. Even if you don't need the information, you should still take the prospect to the area in question or the physical space that will be affected by your product or service. Our intent is to make the prospect comfortable with us, and walking and talking beats sitting there at the kitchen table.

For instance, if you're in the deck business, you will need to shoot grades or make sure that the rear of the home can hold up the header/plate to support the deck. If you are in the room addition or building business, you need to check property lines, and so forth.

Interior products and services are no different. You want to walk and talk versus sitting down at the kitchen table. If you sit down, the prospect will begin to pull you into your product demonstration and you will start talking before you have the necessary information. Move from the front door to the area in question as quickly as possible. This makes the prospect more comfortable with you, and you get the chance to ask great questions while walking around.

Here are a seven key points during this step in the process:

1. When you inspect the space or view the work that needs to be done, it is important to have all the decision makers present.

2. Ask questions; this is the time to show your product/service knowledge, experience, and professionalism. By asking good questions you get the prospects talking and you will most likely pick up key statements and information that will be essential as you move forward with your presentation. Remember, you only learn when the prospects are talking, so get them talking.

3. Take lots of notes. It is essential that you write notes of what the prospects are saying. When prospects see you taking notes, they feel like what they are saying must be important to you and you make them feel important. It is a good idea to ask the prospect "would you mind if I take notes?" This calls attention to the fact that you are listening to what they say and that you are a In-home sales professional.

4. Don't hesitate to make suggestions. When walking the property or inside the home be sure to make intelligent suggestions and give them ideas of things to think about with the project. You can start building value in yourself and your company at this stage by sharing your experience and knowledge through your suggestions. This is a good time to suggest the types of products/service they might need or how they may want to place the product in a certain spot for certain reasons. Make sure you do not talk down to them, as that is the fastest way to find your way back to your car and off their property.

5. Never argue or belittle the prospects. Sometimes they are firm that they want something specific that you might not agree with. Just tell them you can price it both ways and they can make the final decision. Remember, they are the prospects and you are the expert. But they hold the golden key: the checkbook. Arguing with them and making them feel foolish will likely crush your sale.

6. Get them physically involved in the process. If you are using equipment to measure, let them hold one end of the measuring tape. If you are using flags, let them place them. Help them to visualize your product or service.

7. Be observant. This is a great time to bond and look around to see if you have something in common: a race car, show car, horse, tractor, garden, and so forth. Ask them intelligent questions and let them talk about it. Be sincere. Don't be schmoozy, as they will pick up on this, and it will blow your credibility.

DAY 41
In-home Sales Mantra No. 11:
The Concept of a Hot Button

Let me ask you: What is your favorite color? If you said blue, why didn't you say red? Do you like cars or trucks? If you said trucks, why not cars? Do you like sport cars or luxury cars? If you said luxury cars, why not sports cars? Do you like watching baseball or football? If you said baseball, why not football? Do you like to buy expensive items or are you a saver? If you answered that you're a saver, why? The answer is simple: It's one of your *hot buttons.*

What turns your crank may not be what turns the crank of your prospects. When you unlock the ability to find these hot buttons you will find that closing the sale will be a snap. Pretend that the prospect's order is in a locked safe and once you open the safe you will make the sale at any margin you want within reason. Can you imagine this? All you have to do to open that safe is to identify the combination and that combination is the prospect's hot buttons. As you push a button, it unlocks one part of the combination to open the safe. One prospect will have a one-button combination and another may have an eight-button combination. It will be up to you to determine how many buttons it will take to open that safe and get that order. I learned this concept early in the 1990s and my **In-home** sales soared.

Everyone reveals their hot buttons differently. Hot buttons are thoughts and images that touch the senses of your customer. You and your customer have auditory (hearing), visual (seeing), and kinesthetic (touch) senses. Some people are very visual, some are into touching and handling things, and some are into listening. Maybe the words were, "Sally, my brother was in the service and served three tours as a Marine." This might have been a connection or hot button for Sally because her husband, father, brother, or son is in the service right now. It could be a picture you show them of your product or service. That may visually connect with one of their hot buttons. Perhaps you have a product that when someone holds, touches, or uses will connect with one of his/her hot buttons.

How do you find prospects' hot buttons? Ask questions, probe. Even when you ask a question, ask another by saying, "Tell me more" or "How so?" This technique is called layering, like trying to get to the center of a tootsie pop. The outside is good but the inside is even better. How do you get to the center of the tootsie pop? Simple, start with the outer part and move toward the center. Start with one major hot button question and keep moving toward the center, which may be an even more important hot button. Take this example:

In-home sales pro: "Sally, when you decide to get this new bathroom, tell me an important characteristic that you will be looking for in that company."

Sally: "Well, after getting totally jacked around by the basement contractor, John and I want a solid *reputable company with referrals.*"

In-home sales pro: "Sally, I totally can understand that. What exactly happened in the basement project?"

Sally: "Well, they started the job *two months late*. Then when they did start they *left the job three times*. The worse part is they *installed the wrong tile color*."

In-home sales pro: "Unbelievable, not the first time I ever heard a story like this. Let me make a few notes. Reputable referrals are not late, they don't leave the job site, and they don't install the wrong product."

Hot button layer 1: Sally wants a reputable company and referrals.

Hot button layer 2: They were two months late and installed the wrong product.

Of course, when I get to my professional presentation in Step 6, I will address these hot buttons and bring John and Sally's emotional level up and prove to them that not all companies do business like the basement contractor. I am also prepared to prove this to them with referrals and letters.

Think about this today and get prepared for tomorrow.

DAY 42
In-home Sales Mantra No. 12:
Successful Selling Comes
from the Heart

You must believe in every way, shape, and fashion that your company is the best. Selling comes from the heart, and prospects will pick up on the passion you show for your product, your service, your company, and yourself. If prospects sense you care more about them and their needs than you do about getting the sale then you are very close to getting the sale. Demonstrate this by asking questions and taking notes of what they share with you. This will cause them to see that you care about them and you care about their needs. Humor doesn't hurt either. People like salespeople who have a sense of humor, so loosen up.

When you touch your customer's heart you can see how the price seems to be secondary in the decision-making process. For today, treat all people you meet the same way you want to be treated. If someone upsets you, kill the hate with *love*. Try it, it works!

DAY 43
Step 4 Continued:
Visual Inspection, Part 2

In continuing your visual inspection of the prospect's property ... Here are more key points during this process:

1. Dress better and act more professional than the salesperson who was there before you. You are on stage and you want to be better than your competition.

2. Pick up buying signals. This includes questions the prospect asks that include industry buzz words that show they have done some research. Observe the dialogue between the two decision makers to see if they show interest. It also may include their visual response to your comments. Keep a mental note or write down any buying signals that surface during your site visit. A good example might be that Mr. Jones says, "Gosh, I can't wait to get this new deck; we have a graduation party coming up in two months." You may want to reference this statement when you close. It can't get any better than that.

3. Listen for industry terms. Oftentimes a prospect will use a word or phrase that would not be known unless the prospect has spoken to another provider of your product/service. In some cases you may hear a word that is frequently used

by your competitor. In either case make a note and then develop your strategy to address this new knowledge.

4. Continue to identify the prospect's behavioral style. As you walk and talk, you will pick up additional clues as to his/her style.

5. Stay out of arguments. Occasionally the prospects, say a husband and wife, will go at each other about the purchase. Stay clear of this argument and continue to do your work or write notes while looking at the area in question. Do not engage! Observe who is saying what and adjust your approach for the next step. Oftentimes you will pick up buying signals by one of the parties involved.

6. Listen and look for hot buttons. We will get more into hot buttons in the Needs Analysis (Step 5) but remember to listen and look since you will typically get good and accurate hot buttons during the visual inspection step.

Warning: Avoid giving a presentation or too much information in this stage. Prospects may ask you questions about your product or service while you are doing your visual inspection, and the next thing you know you are getting into your product demonstration. For example the prospect may say, "So Ron, can I get this deck in cedar with XYZ Decking?" Respond with, "Mr. Jones, that's a great question. Would you like it in cedar? After we get done with the site inspection I have several pictures and stain colors for you to review. It's a bit windy (or chilly, or warm) out here so I will finish up and we can proceed inside the home, and I will get the pictures and lay them out for you."

Pro In-home Sales Tip: Stay with the 10 steps! Some salespeople say that they can make a sale any time in the sales process when they feel the time is right. Until you are exceeding your sales quota using the 10 Step **In-home** Sales **Continuum**™, I recommend you stay with the flow of the 10 steps. You might be in the prospect's home near the time to ask the closing question, and the prospect wants to go back outside and review the site one more time. If you feel that this is the time to ask the closing question and you're getting buying signals then go for it. You can always go back inside to complete the paperwork. If the prospect wants to go outside and re-measure or take another visual inspection, great! This is a major buying signal.

DAY 44
Step 5: Needs Analysis

This step sets the stage for your presentation and demonstration. During the needs analysis you will identify the prospects hot buttons! You will reflect back during the presentation and demonstration, Step 6, and address the hot buttons you identify in this step. This is the point in the process where you ask a lot of questions, which helps you gather key problems the prospects have experienced in the past, needs they currently have, and how they plan to move forward with the purchase. If you master this step, you will overcome challenge No. 7 from Day 3: not conducting a proper needs analysis.

Let's say you're at the doctor's office because you have been experiencing a massive headache. Upon arrival you are put into an exam room. The doctor walks in. The first thing the doctor asks is your name. You respond. At that point the doctor says, "I understand you have a bad headache" and then says, "Please put this gown on, get on that table, and we'll get you in for surgery." How would you respond?

You would want them to examine you, weigh you, ask you questions about your medical history. You expect the nurse to ask you twenty-plus questions and check parts of your body. You expect the doctor to come in and reconfirm your condition since you don't want mistakes. Your customer has the same desire. They expect you to ask questions and confirm their answers. It shows that you care about them. Step 5 is a key step that many salespeople rush through or eliminate because it feels like hard work. Our goal is to help you develop the questions and the process for this key step so you can execute it flawlessly and with confidence.

We will cover several generic questions and then you will want to work with your team to develop additional questions that are specific to your product or service. Once you have the questions defined, you will put them into one document—what we refer to as the **In-home** Fact Finder. If you have your questions written down and you have your **In-home** Fact Finder in front of you when you are working with a prospective customer, the call will go smoothly and you will progress to Step 6 with the right type of information to secure the sale on the first call.

(For help on your fact-finding questions, go to www.salesoctane.com and hit the In-home link to contact us.)

Following are generic questions used for **In-home** selling. Remember, if they say it, it must be true, and if you say it, it might be doubtful.

- How long have you been thinking of this home improvement?

- When you decide to hire a company, what is your goal for when you want this completed?

- How many bids do you plan on getting? How many so far? (If you asked this earlier just reconfirm.)

- What kind of a budget do you have in mind for this project? What is your hope number?

Here's a sample conversation:

In-home sales pro: "John let me ask you, you are getting a new deck, correct?"

Scenario #1

Prospect: "Yes, we are."

In-home sales pro: "I know you stated earlier you had received two bids. Let me ask you, based on those bids, what budget did you have in mind?"

Prospect: "Well, we would like to be around $15,000."

This is a perfect answer but be on your guard because they may be low-balling you. The last two bids could have been near $20,000. Just keep moving forward and use this data later. Or, they might answer your question about budget this way:

Scenario #2

Prospect: "We don't really have a budget, it depends."

In-home sales pro: "Sure I understand. Let me ask you, what is your hope number? What did you hope the number would be?

Prospect: "Well, we were hoping it would be around $15,000."

In-home sales pro: "Great, is that number the funds you have set aside or the number that fits your budget for monthly installments?

Prospect: "No, we have the funds available."

Other needs analysis questions for your Fact Finder, which you will develop tomorrow in Day 45, are the following:

- Do you have the funds set aside or what, if any, assistance will you need?

- Have you ever seen our product before? If yes what did you like about it?

- How long have you lived in this home? How long do you plan on staying? (This is a good question because it gives you a clue of home equity. If they have been in the house twenty to thirty years, chances are they have good equity and may have a home equity line of credit for the purchase.)

- What is the main purpose for the home improvement?

- What type of experience have you or any of your friends or family members had in the past with this type of home improvement? If they did, ask, "What was the experience like?" (We're not looking for any negativity here, but in the event you get a huge negative story take notes and show empathy.)

- What are the three most important things you are looking for in a company when you decide to hire them for a project like this? (Ask all the decision makers. This question and the next are very important because their answers will give you the information you need to execute the next step.)

- How would you rank those three in terms of most important, second most important, and third? (Ask all decision makers.)

- Which one on the list is the single most important? (Write it down.)

DAY 45
The Fact Finder

As you develop your additional questions for your **In-home** Fact Finder it is important to craft the questions to eliminate a "yes" or "no" answer. We call these open-ended questions. A simple rule is to take your question and recraft it so it begins with a who, what, when, where, why, or how. You may find it necessary and helpful to use a close-ended question at certain times, but keep in mind you don't get much information from a close-ended question. Keep the customer talking by asking open-ended questions.

Make thorough notes when you use the **In-home** Fact Finder. When you write notes you reinforce that what they are saying is important. Second, it buys you time to either decide your next step or look at your **In-home** Fact Finder to identify the next question.

If you are the sales manager or coach, we suggest you create a clean **In-home** Fact Finder and make multiple copies for all your sales professionals. When your sales professionals make or lose a sale, make sure they submit this completed **In-home** Fact Finder to you. This document will let you know if they are asking the right questions. How can we sell or design a product if we don't even know what the prospect wants or needs? In your weekly sales meeting you may want to select a sales professional to role-play this step. By practicing this step, your **In-home** sales professionals will become more natural with the questioning.

If you get resistance from prospective customers, share with them the importance of gathering this information. For example, you may say: "Mr. Jones I need to create a profile on your individual needs so I can make a thorough design that fits your needs. Also, in the event you call me back in a few months I can pull my notes and get re-acquainted with your needs." (Note the "if you call me back"; this is a pressure reliever.) This step cannot be missed or executed haphazardly. Once you practice your **In-home** Fact Finder questions, you will find your prospects will open up and give you all their hot buttons that lead you to the sale .

We have found that some new salespeople cannot conduct a professional **In-home** Fact Finder because of fear, or lack of practice. Some say it's silly and seems kind of sales-ish. Also, we have found that salespeople who feel they cannot ask questions from an **In-home** Fact Finder have an issue with fear. Here's our tip: *Do what you fear.*

PDR stands for *practice, drill, and rehearse.* Go home and practice the **In-home** Fact Finder with your spouse, or anyone you can find who will listen. Do you think doctors practice brain surgery before they actually do one on a living human being? Once you have mastered this step, it will flow smoothly, and the prospects will open up with a tremendous amount of information.

<u>Fact Finding Questionnaire (SAMPLE)</u>

ABC Home Improvement

Prospect Name: _____

Date of Visit:_____/_____/_____

REP:_____

1   How did you hear about ABC?

2   What will the structure mainly be used for?

3   What options were you thinking of?

4   What other options are you considering?

5   What is your budget? What is your hope number?

6   Funds available, or need financial assistance?

7   What permits will you need? Have you requested them?

8   How long have you been considering completing this project?

9   When do you plan to build this structure (create urgency)?

10 When was the last time you did a home improvement? What was that experience like?

11 What are the three most important things you will be looking for when hiring a company to do this project?

    1) _____

    2) _____

    3) _____

Which is the most important? _____

Revised 4/22/08

DAY 46
Framing the Budget
for Your Prospect

If your customers have no idea what their budget is, and do not even have a "hope" number from Day 44/45, then you have to frame the budget for them. This is a simple process once you've practiced it a few times. All you need are the three levels you offer for your product or service: sort of a good, better, and best approach. Once you have those three levels identified, you then put together the price points (budget) for each of those levels. You're now ready to use the framing concept to know whether you really have a qualified opportunity in front of you. If they are not qualified, get out of there.

Here's how it sounds and looks:

In-home sales pro: "John, just so I make sure to price out the right product/service, we have three products/services—A, B and C."

Note: When you are laying out the three options you have to remember to use your hands to visually illustrate that A (which is your highest-priced solution) is on top, B is in the middle, and C is your lowest quality/price. (Whatever you call them or however you define them is up to you. If you need help, go to www.salesoctane.com and go to the In-home tab and contact us.)

Clients will select based on what they feel is their desired range. For example:

Prospect: "I'm thinking B to perhaps C, depending on the price."

In-home sales pro: "Great, John, based on the size of your project, and don't hold me to this number, our 'B product' is going to be about $20,000, and the 'C product' about $17,000. Does that seem like it might fit?" (The budget numbers must be developed for your **In-home** sales professionals by the leadership team.)

Framing is a simple technique to get customers to select a range of solutions, because they don't feel they are committing to a price. Once the customer selects the range of solutions, the **In-home** sales professional simply applies a budget price to the range the customer has selected based on the size of the project. Watch the customers' responses. They will either tell you outright that the price is or is not in the range or will show their discomfort at the price. Don't go into denial. If it appears they are shocked by the number, ask the question: "John, I sense this is more than you wanted to spend. I'm OK with that. You'll remember I mentioned a few minutes ago that I can just as well take a 'no' as I can take a 'yes.' Just let me know."

DAY 47
Step 6: A Professional Presentation Equals a Professional Paycheck

During my 20 years of **In-home** selling experience I have always used a professionally written presentation book during my sales presentation. I have produced and written several books when I found that my employer did not provide one. Having a professional presentation book is absolutely essential to the success of Step 6. A professional book that is offered in a manner consistent with the next several days will keep you from falling victim to challenge No. 8 on Day 3: not knowing how to present the product properly.

The presentation book is your major *value*-building tool. This is your chance to separate yourself from the competition and get the prospect to become a customer. The prospects have set aside the time to meet with you for this presentation so make sure you give them value for their time. The presentation book should be divided into three sections.

Section 1: company history. This is where you build the strength of your organization. If you have been around for a number of years, make sure to emphasize your years in business. If you have a certification (veteran-owned, woman-owned/minority business, etc.) or professional affiliation, make sure to reinforce with a logo from the certification or association. The more visual the better. Use pictures, images, and graphics versus just text. Remember, you will cover this quickly with the prospects so don't have too many pages.

Section 2: why your company is better than the other options. What are the significant differences between your company and the competition? Include these points in this section. Again, pictures speak a thousand words, so use photos, images, or graphics over words wherever possible. This is also where you include your list of references. Blow your own horn here by listing past clients and their glowing remarks about you, your company, and your product/ service. It is even better if you have pictures of the people who made the reference statements. People buy from people they like and they buy from people like themselves. If they see pictures of people just like them who bought from you, they will feel more comfortable making the decision to invest in your product or service. Also make a section at the end of your book for the following:

- Before and after pictures of previous jobs

- Reference page with names and numbers

- Actual pictures of your customers standing by the jobs that were completed.

Section 3: your product or service with features and benefits. Typically, you already have this material in your existing product and service brochures. One note: Always point to the features and benefits that are far superior to that of your competition. Eventually these unique features and benefits will substantiate the additional cost you are charging, so don't fail to focus on them during your presentation.

Also, remember you prepped them outside with the disarming statement: "At any time if my colors or products do not fit your needs, I will be on my way. I can take a no as well as a yes." Now is the moment to show and tell why you and your company are the best.

DAY 48
In-home Sales Mantra No. 13:
People Love to Buy;
They Hate to Be Sold

In-home sales professionals understand and embrace this principle. They work hard to create a selling environment where the prospect feels free to make a buying decision. They work hard to minimize the pressure that causes a prospect to feel like he or she may be making a hasty decision. In short, sales professionals work hard to influence the prospect to buy while eliminating the pressure associated with being sold.

In many ways we are forced into this poor practice. Initially, pressure to meet your sales goals or your personal financial needs may have caused you to push hard for the sale. You may have even been trained to "put the pressure" on the prospect. Whatever the reason, most salespeople begin their career by pushing hard and thus fail to create the long-term relationships with customers that lead to additional sales and referrals. In our effort to try and pressure prospects, we, in fact, make them uncomfortable and suspicious.

There are five techniques you can use to minimize pressure and let the prospect buy:

1. *Approach each sales opportunity as if you don't need the sale.* Sales professionals know that a prospect can sense their desperation. If you go into a sales opportunity by telling yourself,

"I have to get this sale," you are desperate. You will try too hard and the prospect will feel like he or she is being sold. Instead, by telling yourself you don't need the sale, it will cause you to appear less desperate, and the prospect will become more comfortable and less suspicious of your motives.

2. *Ask questions.* That's right, when you ask questions, the prospect talks more and you talk less. The less you talk, the less chance you have to come off as a high-pressure salesperson. The less you talk, the better the chance the prospect will share what he or she is looking for and why he/she wants to buy. The less you talk, the more you learn about the prospect.

3. *Believe that your product or service will have a positive impact on your prospect.* Your prospect will pick up on your confidence in your product, and that will make him/her more comfortable. You may have to invest more time in the short term to learn about your product so you can have that confidence.

4. *Make more calls after you complete a sale.* Success breeds success. When you sell something, your confidence increases, your desperation decreases, and subsequent prospects can sense the difference. That difference will make them more comfortable and willing to buy.

5. *Learn how to adapt to their style.* Commit to memory the techniques so you know how to adapt and when to close based on the behavioral style of the prospect.

Become a In-home sales professional. When you minimize pressure and increase the comfort of the buying experience, your customers will *love* to buy from you. For today memorize this sales motto: "I lead people to make decisions that are right for them."

DAY 49
In-home Sales Mantra No. 14:
Muscle Memory and Practice

I can't stress enough the importance of practice. I love sports, and at the time this book is being written we just ended the 2008 Summer Olympics in Beijing. At times during the televised segments they showed the life and training of a particular athlete. Many of the athletes started their training between the ages of 6 and 11. When someone starts that young in their development of a particular swimming stroke or running style, he or she is developing what is often referred to as muscle memory. Literally, the muscles begin to develop a memory for the correct stroke and the correct stride.

Here's the question for today: What type of muscle memory do you have with your sales techniques? What would have happened if you started sales training at the age of 11 and then at the age of 21 had your first sales call? What if you had been role-playing or developing your skills at handling prospects objections for 10 years before you made your first sales call? If you had that type of muscle memory before you made your first call, just think how prepared or relaxed you would be. We all know it's not possible to go back. You are making a decision by reading this book to develop the muscle memory of an **In-home** sales professional.

For today take a few minutes to identify the sales muscle group that is your weakest. What days in this book do you need to review? Practice will create the muscle memory you need for years to come.

DAY 50
Setting Up the Presentation

Let's put Step 6 into context. You have done everything possible to get all the decision makers at the appointment (thus avoiding the one-legged appointment). Upon your initial greeting, you made a positive first impression and identified the style of your prospect(s). You have adapted your approach based on their style and developed a comfortable rapport with the prospect(s). You quickly moved to the area where the product or service will be used and asked great questions to uncover their hot buttons. You have even offered several valuable insights about their situation or project in order to build your value and credibility. After all that you are positioned perfectly to present your solution based on their hot buttons, their issues, and their statements. Remember, it's not about you, it's about them.

I personally like to get to the kitchen table and make sure I seat everyone where I want them to sit according to this diagram.

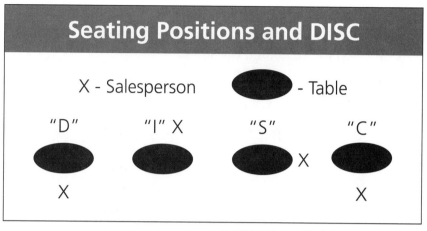

© 2008 Target Training International

It is hard to talk or show pictures outside in the wind, rain, or snow, and the goal is to make this as comfortable for them as well as for you. If they don't let you back in the house something went wrong in previous steps and you need to fix it. I feel that the kitchen is a very comfortable area and beats the dining room or certainly the living room, where you are trying to balance your presentation book on their laps.

It's OK to accept a glass of water, coffee, or tea at this point, if they offer. Occasionally, depending on the area of the country where you work, you may have prospects who offer an alcoholic beverage. Don't fall for this. The **In-home** sales professional never consumes alcohol on a sales call, period. Simply respond, "I have so much to do that I have to refrain, but thank you for your kind offer." This response is gracious and reinforces that you are busy because everyone is buying your product or service.

Follow these important aspects of the presentation:

- Keep the duration of Step 6 to a maximum of 17 minutes. The prospect will lose any information given beyond 17 minutes. People can only retain so much information and so many facts before their mind starts to drift. That's why you sell the sizzle, not the steak.

- Modify your presentation to the prospect's behavioral style, as noted in earlier chapters.

- For today remember what behavioral style he or she is and adapt your presentation.

DAY 51
Stay with the Flow!

Don't get off track or skip pages of your professional presentation. Occasionally you will have prospects who say they don't need this information because they either checked you out on the Internet or they are just impatient. In this case you just go back to bonding or ask more questions. Ask what they saw on the Internet or maybe get off the subject completely, and when you get back to the presentation just pick up at the point you left off. Another option is to tell the prospects you will summarize *just for them* because they are in a hurry. However, continue to cover the same material but appear as if you are moving faster.

Take this example:

Prospect: "I know what your company does so let's skip this and get to the price."

In-home sales pro: "No problem, let me speed up and skip through some of the details on these pages." (But don't skip a page—just appear as though you are moving faster through the pages.)

Maintain control of the presentation book. Never let prospects take your book from you and assume control over you. All the prospects are doing is testing you. They are either in the sales profession themselves or they are control freaks and just want to see your response. Smile and say, "Wow, you're making my job easy."

They will typically slide the book back at you at that point for two reasons. First, control-oriented people do not want to make it easier for you, so when you tell them they are making it easier, they will attempt to regain "control" by literally shoving the book back. Second, if they are in the sales profession, no one is making their job easier, so they feel like they should not give you any favors. In both cases, you get the book back and are in control. Make sure you keep your cool and use wit rather than getting defensive.

Bring it back to their hot buttons. Always address their hot buttons, which you discovered in Step 5. Place your filled-out Fact Finder Questionnaire (FFQ) near your presentation book so you have your notes available as you review the presentation book.

DAY 52
Major Commitments for Minor Questions

A great presentation book creates very few *major* objections or questions. Don't get misled here. *Minor* objections and questions are fantastic, because they show interest in your product or service and in you. If prospects sit there with no questions or comments, you might have lost them or they are probably not interested. However, if you get a question like "Ron can we get that in oak?" then they are sending you a positive signal. It may be their hot button. In this case it is essential that you not answer the question without getting some type of a commitment. There are three typical ways you can answer the question:

1. (Rookie:) "Oh yes, I can get that in oak for you."

2. (In-home sales pro:) "Sally, would you like it in oak?" or "Sally, is oak what you're looking for?"

3. (In-home sales pro:) "Sally, if I could get it in oak, are you ready to move forward today?"

With option 1 you have answered the question, and the prospect is not prompted to respond. This is not an option for the **In-home** sales professional.

With option 2 the customer is obviously going to answer with a positive (if he/she asked the question, he/she must want it in oak); however, the customer will typically give you a buying signal and possibly even some additional information about why he/she wants oak or why he/she asked the question. Perhaps the customer wanted oak and the other competitor did not have oak. Sally may respond with "Yes, oak is what we really want but I wasn't sure you had it available."

With option 2 you received a minor commitment. When you ask, "Is oak what you want/are looking for?" and Sally responds with "yes, we would like oak" then you have gotten a minor commitment. Think of commitments like you would of building a brick wall. One brick does not make a wall. A stack of bricks placed one atop another makes a wall, and the more bricks you have the more substantial the wall. Minor commitments are the same way. With each minor commitment you are building a solid wall that your competitor will not be able to penetrate.

Option 3 is only to be employed once you are in Step 7. For now, get good at always answering your prospect's question with a clarification: "Is that what you're looking for?" or "Is that what you want?"

Minor commitments for hot buttons. As we mentioned on the front cover there are secrets to the one-call close. We will now address one of the major secrets. If you follow the 10 steps in sequence you will get at least 10 minor agreements ("yeses") before you even tell the prospect the price.

If I know from fact finding (Step 5) that I have a few minor objections to overcome, I make sure I blend them right into my presentation. Let's say, for example, that the prospect has mentioned that the project must be completed by the end of the year, December 31, and that this is going to be difficult for everyone if the prospect does not move forward. For example: "Sally, earlier you told me you needed this project done by the end of the year. Since we have multiple crews in our company and build year round, your deadline will not be a problem for us. That will satisfy your needs, won't it?"

Avoid negative selling like the plague. Never slander your competition, period. Never ever slander or make fun of the little guy. If you know your competition is a small local provider say, "Mr./s. Jones, I understand why local folks do what they do for the prices they offer, and I am OK with it as long as they too work with honesty and integrity. We typically find that warranties are only as good as the company backing them." This places concern over warranties in their mind. It also positions your great warranty and your company's ability to service the account long term, which the small company cannot do.

DAY 53
Leverage Your
Competitive Advantage

In most cases your product or service has unique features, benefits, or advantages versus the competition. During your professional presentation you will cover these attributes. It is important that you share them without demeaning your competition. We provide several examples of features, benefits, and advantages of typical **In-home** companies, followed by the salesperson's statement and confirmation question at the end of each example. If you have other significant competitive advantages over your competition and want to address it with prospects, without negative selling, follow this same process.

Your company has the following advantages:

- Your own certified installers. Many of your competitors subcontract the installation but you have your own certified installers.: "We employ our own certified installation crews. We hire them, train them, and certify them so we have consistent trained team members doing our installations. We find that our customers want trained professionals doing their installations. Earlier you mentioned that was important. Is that a consideration in your decision of who to hire?"

- Backed written warranties: "Our warranty is backed by our years of experience. We find our customers are concerned about whether we can back up the warranty. Is there anything else you need to see to confirm how we will handle a warranty claim in the future? Earlier you mentioned this was important. Is this still important to you?"

- Company-approved third-party finance institutions: "We have two to three lenders that can assist you in making this dream possible and affordable. Is financing helpful?"

- In-house customer support call center using our 800 number: "If you ever have a question or concern when you call our offices, you will be connected directly to our own in-house customer service personnel. We do not outsource customer service. We find our customers want to deal directly with us and talk to the same person versus someone new every time they call. Will that work for you?"

- Larger company that is debt free: "Given the size of our company and our years in business, we are debt free. What that means to you is we do not take your deposit and use it to finish someone else's project. That's called floating the deposit and we do not float your deposit. We put your deposit into escrow until the project is complete. We can do that simply because we are debt free. I want to make sure you're comfortable with how we will handle your money. Is working with a debt free company important to you?"

- Fully insured, some with builders risk insurance: "We are fully insured meaning that if something were to happen to any of our team members on your property while completing your project, our builders risk insurance covers them and protects you. In this day and age you never want to be surprised with a personal property claim against your insurance with an uninsured contractor. Does that put your mind at ease?"

If you need additional help identifying how to use your strategic competitive advantages, visit www.salesoctane.com; go to the In-home Sales link and contact us.

DAY 54
The Tie-Down

Make sure you use *tie-downs* and ask open-ended questions targeted at prospects' high-priority hot buttons. Tie downs are confirmation statements that gain you minor agreements from your prospect. Example: "Sally, being a debt-free company, in business over 40 years, seems like a stable company, wouldn't you agree?" You do not want to do this with each and every feature, benefit, and advantage you cover; however, with the high-priority hot buttons it is important to tie the hot buttons down.

For example: "Sally, earlier I asked you to name what you were looking for when hiring a company to do this project, and you replied, a solid reputable company. Now that I told you we have been in business for 29 years and are a debt-free company, this probably makes you feel at ease doing business with us, doesn't it?" We use prospects' hot button information to turn around and let *their own words* sell our product. After all, they gave you the information on their own. We just took notes as they gave us their hot buttons in Step 5 and then fed it back to them during the book presentation in Step 6, and now we tie them down with their high-priority hot buttons.

During Steps 1–5 you will identify several hot buttons from your prospects. They may have said that they had been burned in the past by a disreputable contractor and wanted to make sure they went with a stable company on this project. During Step 6 it is important to circle back around to that hot button and tie them down.

Begin by reminding them that you listen by restating their concerns/hot buttons. For example: "Mr. Jones, when we were outside you informed me that it's important to you that you do business with a stable company, not one like the company that did the windows in your last house, is that correct?" If they said it earlier, they will most likely say, "Yes, that's correct." Now tie them down with how your company, product, and service will address the concerns that they just confirmed. For example, "Mr. Jones, XYZ Home Improvement is a 45-year-old company. We have installed more than 25,000 decks in that time period and we are debt free. Being debt free and 45 years in business, with over 25,000 installations, surely meets that requirement, Mr. Jones, wouldn't you agree?"

If he says, "Yes, Ron, I agree," then you have tied them down. He said it, so it must be true!

Always have your Fact Finder information sitting right next to your presentation book so that you don't miss the hot buttons you wrote down from Step 5. As you become an experienced **In-home** sales professional, you will have the ability to remember their hot buttons and spin them back at the right point in the presentation. This takes practice and muscle memory.

In-home Pro Sales Tip:: Tape it! You should not even think about going on your first appointment unless you have practiced your professional presentation and videotaped yourself doing the presentation. You need to watch yourself on the video to understand how you look, how you sound, and how your body language works. Given the fact that the professional presentation should be done in less than 17 minutes, this should be an easy process to tape, review, and retape, review, etc. Remember Perfect Practice Makes Perfect and Permanent!

If during the professional presentation you lose one of the decision makers because the phone rings, someone's at the door, the dog needs to be let out, or the children need to be dealt with, pause and wait for them to return. It's risky to let one of the parties miss good information. Use your wit and personality; perhaps ask for a glass of water while the other person is away. Do whatever it takes to make sure you have everyone back at the table before you proceed.

The worst case scenario is when someone has to leave right then and there. Perhaps they received a call and had to run and get the children right away. Whatever the reason, you need to stick to the 10-step system. We know it takes both decision makers to say yes, so stop your presentation and do not deliver the price. Remember the price is your last ace in the hole. Once the price is out you can't backpedal. If you give the price to one of the decision makers and they say, "Thanks, when Sally gets home I'll talk it over with her and get back to you," then you are cooked.

Another secret of the one-call close is to have all the decision makers there before you cover your pricing. If one has to leave, the best thing to do is reschedule the appointment. Tell them that you want to go back to your office and work on a few more possible designs and make sure everything is priced correctly. Tell them you have a couple of other thoughts and want to go back and confirm with your team/president, etc.

This is a good time to address the difference between objections and conditions. Objections are your friends and are good. When they arise during any of the steps, it shows customers are interested in your product or service. If they sit there like road kill, you are not in a good position. Every possible objection on earth can be handled. However, conditions are not your friend. Here are several examples of conditions that will derail the sale:

- They don't have the ability to come up with the money necessary to complete the sale. Better prequalifying from Day 12 will help to avoid this issue.

- They don't have access to the money via credit lines or credit rating that is necessary to complete the sale. Better prequalifying from Day 12 would help to avoid this issue.

- Things are out of your control, such as not being able to get the exact color or brand they want, no matter how hard you try. If you are getting a certain condition over and over again, which is causing you to lose sales, you need to address it in your product or service offering or you need to bring it up sooner in the 10-step sales process, most likely in Step 2, in the prequalifying stage when you are setting the appointment.

- They can't obtain a permit or they need a variance. You should be able to identify that in Step 2.

- They need to purchase a home or land before they can buy your product or service.

DAY 55
In-home Sales Mantra No. 15:
Control the Controllables

You are over half way through the book and have inevitably run into some roadblocks. Challenges and roadblocks are a fact of life. Some challenges in life are out of your control and others are in your control. The thought for today is to *control the controllables.*

Put simply, you will drive yourself crazy blaming or complaining about the things you cannot control. Whatever life throws at you, do not ask the question "Why?": "Why is this happening to me?" "Why do I live here?" "Why did I have these parents?" The list will go on forever and you will never get a satisfactory answer. Instead of asking "Why?" ask "How?" and "What?": First answer the "how" question: "How did I get here?" "How did this happen?" "How did I find myself in this situation?" and make sure you write out your thoughts. Oftentimes you will find there was either nothing you could do about it or you will find out that some of the problem was the result of something you did. Then answer the "What?" question: "What can I do about it?" "What should be my response?" "What should I do the next time?" "What do I have to avoid?"

"Why" questions turn you into a victim and cause you to blame. "How" questions help you identify how you got into the situation. "What" questions help you to control the controllables and move forward. Control the controllables and move forward today. In-home sales professionals cannot afford a lot of baggage.

DAY 56
In-home Sales Mantra No. 16:
Winners Are Losers Who Get Up and Try Again

If you've ever watched the Rocky Balboa movie series, you undoubtedly remember the scene when Rocky is being confronted and challenged by his son. The son tells his aged father, "Please don't fight again, you can't win and you're too old." Rocky replies, "It's not about winning or losing; it's not about how many times you get knocked down. What it's about is how fast you get back up!"

With **In-home** sales you have the daily challenge of being rejected by prospective customers in their homes. Rejection is just a way of life for the **In-home** sales professional. The question is not *if* you are going to be rejected—it will happen. The better question is: What are you going to do *when* you are confronted with rejection? Will you take it personally and give up? If you set your mind to continue to push forward regardless of the rejection, you will continue to get up and try again.

When you've been knocked down and you want to give up, when you think the grass is greener on the other side, when you think you've got nothing left—get up, shake it off and move on. You are a winner. All you have to do is get up and try again. A wise man once told me these words, "All people on earth are winners; it's just that the losers don't know it yet."

DAY 57
Step 7: The Trial Close

You are now on Step 7 of the 10 Step **In-home** Sales **Continuum**™. You have generated a lead yourself or received one from your company (the gift). You have set the appointment within 24 hours and properly qualified the opportunity, making certain all the decision makers will be present. When you arrived, you created a great first impression, built rapport, identified their behavioral styles and adapted your approach. You did a visual assessment of the proposed project, took comprehensive notes, and asked key questions. You conducted a complete and thorough needs analysis and created value by offering some suggestions and uncovering their hot buttons. You asked all the questions from your Fact Finder, noting their responses and all their hot buttons. And finally you did a professional presentation of your solution and tied them down with their own hot button statements.

That's a lot of work you did. Now it's time to get a return on your investment. It's time to test the water to see how close you are to the sale. As discussed earlier, you never move to the next step until the previous step is completed, and nowhere is that more important than Step 7. You are always in control of the meeting and the prospect as long as you stay with the 10 Step **In-home** Sales **Continuum**™. Never design or provide a price for the product/

service (Step 8) without completing the trial close. In other words, complete Step 7 before you go to Step 8.

Getting the Commitment at the Emotional Peak

At this point in the sales call the prospects' personal and emotional levels are at their highest peak. They have invested time with you, which translates to obligation. They are obligated because they have taken your time, and because they have taken their time. Why would they send you away at this point if they just spent (x minutes) of their valuable time with you? The prospects are ready for a design/layout so they can see how this will look in/ on their home. They also want to know the answer to the big question, "How much is this going to cost?" By building that emotion to its peak level and then asking the trial close, you improve the probability of a one-call close.

It's here in Step 7 you will find out whether you did a great job or a less than great job with Steps 1 through 6. If you have been *value building* along the way and gotten several minor "yes" responses with tie-downs, you are perfectly positioned for Step 7. All the doors behind you are now closed up to this step.

Two Trial Close Questions

The **In-home** Sales **Continuum**™ trial close question simply asks the prospects if they have any reason they would not buy from you other than the price of your product or service. It goes like this:

Option No. 1: "John and Sally, based on me and my company alone, other than price, is there any other reason XYZ Flooring could not earn your business?"

Another version adds one key word at the end.

Option No. 2: "John and Sally, based on me and my company alone, other than price, is there any other reason why XYZ Flooring could not earn your business *today*?"

Either trial close question will work. Option No. 2 pushes the trial close more than the first. You will have to try both and determine which option works better for you. Ask the question and stop talking!

Once you ask the question, you must pause, not say another word, and look them in their right eye (which is to your left). Ninety-nine percent of the time the prospect will say, "I don't see any reason at all. How much is it?" or "I like you and your product. I see no problems. I guess it comes down to dollars and cents."

"No" is good here! This will be one of the first times you are going to get a "no." But in this case the "no" is what you're looking for: "No, we don't see any reason at all." Until you get a positive answer you cannot proceed to Step 8. It is at this point you respond, "Thank you, I appreciate the positive feedback. Now, let's design this (the product) and I will get you that price you've been waiting for."

Once they respond with "No, I can't think of anything—other than the price," they can never come back with any type of objection in the end such as:

- We don't like your product.

- We don't like your colors, etc.

- We don't like you.

- We don't like your company.

- We don't like your company history.

- Your product does not fit our needs.

All doors are now closed from Steps 1 to 7 and you can proceed.

If They Object

In the event you get an objection, such as those covered in the list, now is the time to handle it before you invest your time with a design, layout, and pricing activity. Almost 100 percent of the time the prospects say "no" at this point because they did not understand the question or the prospect may think it is a trick question.

In-home sales pro: "John and Sally, based on me and my company alone, other than price, is there any other reason why XYZ Flooring could not earn your business *today*?"

John: "Well, we need to see the price, Ron; we're not making a decision today."

In-home sales pro: "Oh John, I understand, I was not asking you to make a purchase right now. Let me restate the question. I was basically asking, other than price, do you approve of me, my company, and its product line?"

John: "Oh yes, you're doing a great job, and the company seems fine."

In-home sales pro: "Perfect, that's what I was looking for. So basically when I am done with the design and tell you how much, the price would be the only thing holding us back?"

John: "Well, yes, I guess it all comes down to the price."

In-home sales pro: "Of course, you're just like me, you want the best value for the dollar spent. Well, let's move on to that design. At this point, we know you approve of me and my company/product so let's get this in your budget, fair enough?"

John: "Fair enough, let's see the design and I am anxious on the price."

The trial close is one of the most important steps in the 10 Step **In-home** Sales **Continuum™**. Miss it and it will haunt you in the end. The secret of the one-call close involves getting minor agreements along the way. In fact, up to this point in the sale, Step 7, you should have received a positive stimulus at least nine times, and now the trial close is another. We have one last minor agreement at the design step, Step 8, before the price delivery. Get these minor agreements and watch the sale fall into your lap.

DAY 58
Step 8: Design/Layout:
Building Up Your Design

Think about a large **In-home** product/service purchase you've made in your life. Maybe it was a remodeling project in your kitchen. Maybe you finished off your basement. Perhaps you added a deck or a third stall to your garage. If you've ever made an **In-home** purchase, it would have included picking out colors, materials, finishes, and the layout. Step 8, the design step, is the most exciting part in the 10 Step **In-home Sales Continuum™** because this is where the *prospects take ownership*. By now they have heard your story. They have also told you that, other than price, they are ready to buy your product/service from you. You have most likely gotten their budget, or their "hope" number so you know what you are aiming for.

There is a good chance that if you are an **In-home** salesperson you do not have the luxury of bringing your product to your prospects' home. You can bring samples, colors, pictures, videos, and brochures, but you can't literally place your prospective client in the finished product/solution. It would be great if there was a virtual world, so they could know exactly how your solution would look in their house. Because we don't have that ability, Step 8 is all about the next best thing: getting your prospects emotionally involved to the point where they "own" the solution. If you have confidence in your product and you know how to design and price it, you will overcome challenge No. 9 from Day 3: not having confidence in your product or pricing.

First things first: Do not proceed to a design stage (Step 8) unless you have completed Step 7.

Tell them what to expect. Inform the prospects that the drawing/layout is a very important step because you and your company don't believe in any hidden costs. For example: "Sally and John, this design step is very important because our company takes pride in the fact that we do what we say we are going to do. What we design here together is exactly what I am going to price and will be exactly what we will place/build in your home/backyard." In the construction world hidden cost is one of the top consumer complaints.

For example, a sales representative misquotes the job, but the job was bid so tight that the company won't eat the mistake, so it sends the sales rep back to the home to ask for more money. The owners are stuck because either they really want the product/service but now have to get more money, or the project has already started and they feel forced into staying with the contractor. Both of these situations sour the customers to your product/service and pretty much eliminate the opportunity to get referrals. The **In-home** sales professional makes it his or her business to correctly price their product or service and eliminate hidden costs. This ensures referrals and keeps you out of costly lawsuits.

DAY 59
Selling the Dream

Use every computer drawing or manual drawing aids you have access to in order to demonstrate a clear visual of what the customer is to receive. Most customers are more visual than they are auditory. Don't just tell them what it will look like—engage them visually. You may not be an artist but take your time and learn how to illustrate your product/service, especially if you are in a big ticket sale. In 1988, before the advent of computer-aided drawing tools, I sold wood decks and used graph paper and colored pencils to illustrate bushes and trees, etc. My drawings literally came to life and placed the prospects in their backyard with the new deck. They could see themselves entertaining others or relaxing with the newspaper. It works!

You can always go down but you can't go up. Always build the dream and add the bells and whistles during the design/layout phase. Remember, if you have built in lots of bells and whistles, when you ask for the order and you get the objection that your price is too high, you can use the "take-away close." (See Appendix A-6). You can remove some of the bells and whistles and still have a chance of getting the product/service in their budget and secure the sale on the same call. During the Fact Finder process (Step 5) you identified their budget or hope number. Your goal is to take away bells and whistles to hit their number before simply lowering your margin. Always hold your integrity and hold your margin.

I compare this analogy to the auto industry. I have several friends that either sell automobiles or own an auto dealership. They know that the top sales professionals work from the retail sticker price down and the weak sales people work from the cost up. When they work from cost and are trying to go up, it is like pushing a rope up a hill. You also leave yourself no room to go down unless, of course, you plan to go out of business. Build in all the bells and whistles and sell the dream. You can remove them later to secure the sale.

DAY 60
The Yes/No List

Put a yes and no column on the drawing for reference. (see the sample at www.salesoctane.com, In-home sales downloads.)

This is how you will use the column to position your close in Step 9.

If you plan to price your product while you are in the home, you can use the yes column as a reference for pricing and then check each of the prospects requested options on the yes side of the list as the prospect confirms their desire for each option. If your pricing structure includes hundreds of options or accessories, this is a great way to avoid costly mistakes. This also reinforces to the prospects that you pay attention to details. You may even say, "I'm going to keep a yes/no list going of what you want me to include so I make sure I don't miss anything."

In the event the prospect must wait several days to make a decision, then you are set when the prospect calls you back. You can refer back to the design with the yes/no list and pick right up where you left off. If you price it and then have to return later because you were unable to close the sale on the first visit then the yes/no list will be very helpful. On the subsequent call when the prospect wonders why a particular bell or whistle is not included in the project or price, you can refer back to the design and say, "My apologies, Sally, here's our design from our meeting and I have X in the NO column, I must have misunderstood you." Never argue or make the prospect look foolish or like a liar.

Confirm that the prospects want what you designed. Do not go to Step 9 (price delivery) without these words: "John and Sally, here is the final design that you and I created. Is this what you visualize in your backyard/house?" You cannot give a price until they have confirmed the design. Make sure you get confirmation from all the decision makers. This is the point where you will receive the last and final minor agreement before the price delivery; by now, you should have received 10 of them.

Two Last Items

Always watch for buying signals. Throughout this entire step, as you are completing the design, you should get buying signals. Watch the wife and husband actually take over and guide you as you do your drawing. This is a buying signal! I love watching one of the decision makers tell me to place X here and X there and the other decision maker says, "No, no, not there, put it here." These are great signals of ownership. Be a master in your design skills and keep the process moving and interactive. Don't bore them or lose their interest. If you are getting resistance or they are not engaged during the design step, you may have blown Steps 3 through 6. Improve your skills in the previous steps, and Step 8 will secure the sale.

If they offer you food or drink (no alcohol), take it, relax and have fun when you design. There is a good chance that the previous salesperson did not conduct a professional job like you are doing.

If you are not able to pin down the design and move to the closing process in Step 9, then make sure to secure the next appointment. Avoid saying you will get back to them after you return to the office and get the necessary information. Secure the second appointment before you leave and make sure that all the decision makers will be present at the subsequent appointment. Remember, if you return to your office and you find out you cannot get the information in time for the appointment you just set, you can always change it. However, if you don't set the appointment, then when you call back to ask what dates will work, it is much easier for the prospects to say they are now all set—with your competitor!

Never leave your design. In the event you do not close the sale on this call, don't leave your design and allow the prospect to give it to the next salesperson from your competition. They may see this as an opportunity to just fax or e-scan the drawing to a competitor for a fast and easy price quote. If a sale is not made and they ask for a copy of the design, simply say this is your master copy and you would be happy to get them one later. After a few days pass and they call you, respond back with "I wanted to swing by and drop it off. I will be in your area on Friday." You want to get back in the door! If they don't call you then make sure you call them and offer to drop it off. You will see in Step 9 that once you present your price to the prospect, you are either going to get a "yes" (you closed), "no" (objection) or "maybe" (the stall), and we will show you how to move the "no" and "maybe" to a closed sale.

DAY 61
Step 9: Closing—Yes, No, or Maybe

This is the moment both you and the prospect have been waiting for. At this point in the 10 Step **In-home** Sales **Continuum™** you have been in the home between one and two hours. You have kept control of the sales call from Step 1 right on through the trial close, and the customers have confirmed that, other than price, there is no other reason they would not move forward with you (Step 7). In Step 8 you worked hard alongside the prospects so they owned the design, and then you had them confirm they want the design that was created (Step 8). Now you want to deliver the price and close. While every step in the **In-home** Sales **Continuum™** must be followed, the closing step is the way you bring it all together. Master this step and you will avoid challenge No. 10 from Day 3: not knowing how to close.

As an **In-home** sales professional, you must avoid the words "bid," "quote," or "estimate." Order takers use these words, and a rookie will say, "Oh, John, I have an estimate for you of $13,000." You, however, are a sales closer, a true **In-home** sales professional. Start converting words from here on out, such as the following:

Negative words	Convert to
Contract	Agreement
Down payment	Initial installment/investment
Sale/sold	Investment
Pitch	Professional presentation
Monthly payment	Monthly installments/investment
Payment	Installment
Will you buy today?	Can we move forward today?
Sign here	Authorize here
Sale/Deal	Get people happily involved

Phrases the in-home sales professional never uses

Your total bid is ...

I brought an estimate with me today of . . .

I have a quote here for you.

I have a rough number of . . .

Can we write this up today?

Are your ready to buy now?

The price is the investment required for the prospects to transform their current situation into the dream they just designed. At this point they can literally begin enjoying the benefits of your product or service with one word: yes!

After you've worked up your total investment figure simply say, "OK, based on what you designed and the options you've chosen, the total investment of your project is . . ." and lay it on the line. Then ask for the order using a preprinted price delivery form (see sample at www.salesoctane.com, In-home sales downloads). You select the alternate choice option that works with your product or service. At this point ask them if easy financing is the way they want to go or if they prefer the cash option. Although there are many other ways to ask for the order, it is important to reinforce that this is their design and you used their options to develop their total investment figure.

Two Types of Closes

A close is defined as helping people make decisions that are right for them. You must close with empathy and lead them. Without the ability to ask for a decision, everyone loses. Your company loses profit and a customer, your customer loses the opportunity to work with you, and your company and you lose as well because you're not getting paid and you lose future referral opportunities.

The two types of closes are the following:

1. *Verbal close.* Alternate of choice/assumption close using a preprinted form. Simply ask the prospect "Would you like to get started this week or next?" (alternate of choice close) or "So, when you would like to get started?" (assumption close).

ABC COMPANY

- Over 15,000 installations
- 40 years in business
- Licensed, bonded and insured

- Written warranties
- In-house installers
- Choice of colors

Investment: Valid For:

Published List Price $_____   30 days

Current Discount & Savings (-) $_____

Adjusted Price $_____   Today's Price

Cash option

50 % at ORDER $_____

50 % FINAL $_____

Easy Credit

No money down at ORDER $_____

Monthly NOTE: $_____

Up to 120 month term.

Rates start at 8.99 percent

No pre payment penalty

No loan fees

"The value Builders"

2. *Written close.* An actual written agreement. When you finish filling out your form, turn it around and deliver your final closing question, "Mr. and Mrs. Jones, with your authorization right here we can move forward." Turn the agreement around, hand them the pen and be quiet.

Three Answers

No matter what technique you use to deliver the price, you will always get one of three answers:

1. "Yes, we will take it!" With the 10 step In-home Sales **Continuum**™ this answer will be most common.

2. "No, we are not interested." If you get this response, you missed something in steps 1-8.

3. "Maybe." This is a very common response, and learning to handle this properly will take you over and beyond your income expectations.

Let's break each of these down.

1. *Yes, we will take it!* "Yes" is the ultimate goal. If after delivering the total investment figure to your prospect you get a "yes," then move to the paperwork and finish the process. You have flawlessly executed Steps 1 through 9 of the 10 Step **In-home** Sales **Continuum**™, and you are on your way to wealth and security. When the customers say "yes," don't look surprised but just say, "Thanks! I sensed you were ready to move forward. Let me confirm the details for our paperwork."

2. *No, we are not interested.* Getting "no" is rare but could happen. If you did a proper trial close (Step 7), you reduce the possibility of getting a "no." In theory, the only "no" you can get at this point is because they feel your price is too high. Any

other "no" means that the prospect lied at the trial closing question. If the price is too high and you smoke that out, then you need to convert a "no" to a "maybe." Following are some examples:

Prospect: "No, we are not interested at this time." Or "leave your card and I'll get back to you."

In-home sales pro: "OK John, I understand this investment is $15,250. Are you saying, 'Ron, not now'?"

Prospect: "Yes, we need to think about it."

(You converted the "no" to the "we need to think about it.")

In-home sales pro: "OK, John, I understand. One question before I leave: Earlier, when I asked you, other than price, could I earn your business, you replied, 'I don't see any other reason, and based on that it can't be me or my company. Would it be fair to assume the price came in a bit more than you were expecting?" (Don't pause here.) "I mean, I was at $15,250. Did you think it was going to come in at around $15,000 even?" (Don't give yourself a huge price gap here, and then shut up!)

Prospect: "Well, yes, it was more than we thought; we were expecting it to be around $14,000."

In-home sales pro: "Great, we are not that far apart. Was that based on anything factual like a magazine article or another bid?"

Prospect: "Yes, another bid." (Perfect, this is the information you were looking for.)

In-home sales pro: "Very good, before I leave, let me take a peek at the other bid to make sure that it is apples to apples in design and material." (Saying "before I leave" drops the temperature in the room.)

If they get out the competitors bid, you're in good shape. If they don't, either they are lying about the $14,000 bid or they are just trying to get rid of you. Once you review the competitor's information, the first step is to make sure it is similar in design and options to your bid. If you're higher but your design is better, then you have done a great job reviewing and you need to bring this to the prospects' attention. Of course, at that point you will make another attempt to close.

3. *Maybe.* Some prospects just don't have the funds or the ability to obtain financing. Sometimes maybe means "not now." We can reduce this problem with proper prequalifying the lead (Step 1). I have come to a conclusion in my 20-plus-year career: I can't sell to people who do not have the financial wherewithal to purchase my goods/services. If someone cannot get a loan, these are conditions, not objections. I am OK with that and blame myself for poor prequalifying. Conditions are situations you cannot control or overcome. Maybe the prospects cannot get a permit or adequate funds or have a low credit score. It is possible they have only a portion of the selling amount saved or loan approved. You need to find this out and overcome it. We address conditions versus objections in more depth on Day 68.

The key to getting a "maybe" is to make sure it's not a stall or a polite way of getting rid of you. Again, as we said previously, you must convert everything to "We need to think about it" and then to the next step, "price." Remember it's always about price.

DAY 62
In-home Sales Mantra No. 17:
Love the Word "No"

Fact: You're going to get way more "nos" than "yeses." For the **In-home** sales professional, the word "no" or the phrase "I/we need to think about it" are going to be a part of your life from here on out. It's much like trying to get a date at the high school dance. You walk up to someone and ask them to dance, and he/she responds "no." You have a choice. You can go home without a dance or you can ask another person to dance. If you keep asking and ask more often, it's just a matter of time, statistically, before you will have a dance. In his book *What You Fear Is What You Become*, Dr. David Thompson writes about the reality that whatever you fear eventually will overtake you and lead you to experience the very thing you are running away from.

Back to the dance floor: Let's say you ask a couple of people to dance and they both respond with "no." You experience rejection twice, so you decide that this hurts and you stop asking people to dance. You stopped because of the fear of rejection. As you head home that evening without a date, you should ask yourself the question, "What do I have?" The answer is no date and a load of rejection, the very thing you were hoping to avoid. If you had continued to ask people to dance, facing your fear of rejection, eventually you would have secured a dance! Facing your fear is the only way to improve your situation.

Remember that you will experience the word "no" on a regular basis. Don't take it personally and continue to ask. Face your fear! Learn to get comfortable with rejection and you will avoid challenge No. 11 from Day 3: not being able to handle rejection.

DAY 63
In-home Sales Mantra No. 18:
We Are Not in the Be-Back Business

This mantra will be a favorite of your company owner or sales manager. In my 20-plus years, a high majority of sales manager and owners of In-home companies want to close on the first visit. There are two main reasons for this:

1. We know that people buy on emotion and back it up later with logic. We also know that the emotional peak is right after the professional presentation (Step 6). So why not close the sale when the buying/emotional level is at its peak?

2. With the cost of leads and fuel, it makes sense to get the prospects out of the market as quick as possible. Even when they say they need to go see their banker, you need to leave the home with a signed agreement and a sufficient deposit. (See Appendix A4)

Today I want you to look back at all the opportunities you lost in the last three to six months prior to reading this book. I bet you have several prospects that did not even return your call. They said they would get back to you, but they never do. Sit back and think of all those who made broken promises.

In-home Pro Sales Tip:: When you're in the prospect's home ask yourself are you selling them, or are they selling you? Sell your prospects on the first visit!

Ask yourself this question: Are you a sales closer or a professional visitor? The choice is yours.

For today, write "I am not in the be-back business." Place this note on your bathroom mirror and in your car. Read it just before you enter a property attempting to make a sale. Be prepared for the prospect to give you more than one objection. Also in your vehicle have in writing all the possible objections that you could get from a prospect, then have all the answers written down underneath each possible objection. *Be prepared.*

DAY 64
Closing Techniques for
the Steady/Amiable

The closing approach for both the Steady/Amiable and the Compliant/Analytical styles is very similar. We address a few minor differences these next two days, but there are more similarities than differences.

Earlier we discussed the characteristics of a prospect with a Steady/Amiable behavioral style. We mentioned that they are the most difficult to identify because they have low emotions and non-demonstrative behavioral styles. The Influencer is talkative, optimistic, and spontaneous (easier to identify). The Driver is impatient, direct, and bottom-line oriented (easier to identify). The Compliant is analytical, questioning, and detail oriented (easier to identify). The Steady is, well, steady! This lack of excessive behavior carries over to the way they make decisions. They move deliberately and are very patient throughout the sales process. Depending on your behavioral style, this may either line up perfectly with your approach *or* this will cause you anxiety as it takes much longer than you would expect. The following techniques will move the sale to a close as fast as possible.

Begin by closing from the first appointment. The first time you meet you want to begin closing. The Steady will take longer than the other styles, especially if your product or service is a change from what they are currently using. You will need to move the sale along using every approach mentioned in this section on each appointment. That's what we mean by closing from the first appointment.

Get incremental agreements throughout the sale. Right from the beginning you want to ask questions such as "How does that look?" or "Is this right?" or "Is this what you're looking for?" Don't expect a highly emotional confirmation. Simply getting them to agree and confirm that what you shared with them looks good will move the sale forward. They are very loyal and consistent. Even a simple agreement becomes an obligation later in the sale.

Take the servant approach. When they respond affirmatively to your incremental agreements, then ask how you can serve them going forward. "What would you like me to do next?" or "What would you like to see next?" are great questions aimed at getting them comfortable with you so they will make the purchase.

Credible comparisons. Be prepared to show how your solution is a bargain compared with your competition. *Do not* negative sell! Share credible comparisons that are meant to show how your offer is the best value.

Don't push. Their relaxed, passive, deliberate approach to decisions requires that you also maintain a similar approach to the sale. You will sense their resistance to strong-arm tactics so avoid them at all costs. The extra patience and effort on your part will be repaid with a loyal, long-term customer. Their resistance to change will also work for you when a competitor comes knocking.

Create a "bargain" tipping point. The Steady appreciates a bargain so if you have a "limited" offer you can use this to re-engage and keep the sales process moving forward. Make sure your approach is passive and professional versus aggressive, forceful, and cheap.

Don't run once you close. When the Steady decides to purchase, he or she is still in the decision-making process. Confirm they've made the right decision by taking time to share with them how you will implement their order, installation, etc. After you thank them for their order and placing confidence in you, take a few minutes to share the details of implementation. This will secure their confidence in you and their decision to buy from you.

Give details, details, details. Given the fact that Steady customers rarely get into great detail, you may not have given them a lot of detailed information during the sale. Make sure to provide them the detailed information as a "take-away." Often there is another party involved with the purchase (could be someone who uses the product, created the specification, or ultimately has to sign the check for your product/service), and he/she may not be a Steady. These other folks may want to see the detailed information, and when they begin to question the Steady, the sale may be put on hold, or worse, cancelled. By providing the detailed information as a follow-up and calling the Steady prospects' attention to the fact that you've given them the information "in case someone wants to see the particulars," you've decreased the probability of them backing out of the sale.

Apply reasonable, consistent follow-up. If you did not get the order, then share with them what you will do next so there are no surprises. Make the calls with low-pressure statements: "Just checking in," "Want to make sure you have everything you need," and "If you have any questions please feel free to give me a call" are examples of the approach that works. If they've shared with you they have a pressing date or time frame, then use this in the follow-up: "I want to make sure we hit the tight time frame you shared with me."

For today write a few of the statements you would ask and strategies you could use for your product or service from each of the steps listed. Identify a prospect with a Steady behavioral style and use these techniques as soon as possible. Remember, practice makes permanent!

DAY 65
Closing Techniques for
the Compliant/Analytical

The Compliant/Analytical style is marked by a cautious, systematic, and exacting approach to decisions. They are known for very thoughtful decisions, having weighed all the evidence. The sales professional must approach the Compliant/Analytical with a careful, linear, and accurate presentation in order to improve the probability of closing the sale. Depending on your behavioral style, this approach may feel very foreign and slow. It's worth the extra effort because the Compliant/Analytical is a very loyal customer. They also make great referrals because everyone knows they do their homework. It's worth the effort!

The first time you meet you want to begin closing. The Compliant will take longer than the other styles, especially if your product or service is a change from what he/she currently uses or if your product or service is unknown or untested. You will need to move the sale along, using every approach mentioned in this section on each appointment. That's what we mean by closing from the first appointment. The following techniques will move the sale to a close as fast as possible:

Get incremental agreements—extreme version. Right from the beginning, you want to ask questions such as "How does that look?" or "Is this right?" or "Is this what you're looking for?" Don't expect a highly emotional confirmation. Simply getting them to agree and confirm that what you shared with them looks good and responds to what they are looking for will move the sale forward. The goal here is to get the prospects talking. Whereas both the Steady and Compliant are more introverted than extroverted, the Steady is more people oriented, while the Compliant is all about tasks, details, and analysis. You need to draw each test-close response out of them by asking extreme questions, such as "Have I given you *everything* you need?" "Is there *any* other information you need?" and "Have I answered *all* your questions about this feature?"

Use options. Similar to the Driver, the Compliant does not like to be painted into a corner. Therefore, giving them only one option feels a bit like they are in the corner, and you'll notice them being evasive when you go for the close. By offering them two to three options, you can identify which option they are leaning toward and move them closer to the sale.

Detail the cost justification. Be prepared to show how the product or service is "cost-justified." As you share the compelling analysis, use an incremental agreement trial close to make sure they are still tracking down the path toward a sale. If not, don't go into denial. Regroup, get the correct information, and get back in front of them.

Listen to and watch each response. Before asking for the order, you want to be confident that you've given them what they asked for and have answered all their questions. If they respond to one of your incremental agreement questions with a half-committed "well … yeah, I think so," the answer is a resounding *no*. Immediately confirm that it appears there is something else they might need. Don't go into denial. If they do not have all the information they need, when you ask for the order, they will "want to get back to you" (code for "I'm going to have to keep looking"). You lose, they lose, everyone loses. Listen to and watch each response and adjust accordingly.

Share "the one downside." Although not a frequently used approach, this often works with extremely evasive and cautious prospects with a Compliant behavioral style. Because of their cautious nature, they may be suspicious of your non-stop positive and optimistic statements about your product or service. If you have a "downside" that you know is not going to be a problem for them, you can share it as "the one downside." By offering the one downside, you gain credibility because you're just like them—wanting to evaluate the pros and cons! Again, only offer this if you know it is not going to be a problem in their situation.

Create a tipping point. If there's any deadline or time-sensitive consideration that might help to expedite the order, then share that information in a non-confrontational manner. Tell them you want them to make sure you "deliver on time" or want to make sure they "take advantage of the discount," for example.

Do not push, let them direct you to the close. Ask the question "What's the next step?" and oftentimes they will tell you the specific step to close the sale. If they are not ready and want more information, then identify how and when you will get the additional information to them and ask, "Once I get that information to you what's the next step after that?"

Don't run once you close. Similar to the Steady, when the Compliant decides to purchase, he/she is still in the decision-making process. After you thank them for their order and/or placing their confidence in you, confirm they've made the right decision by taking time to share with them how you will implement their order, installation, etc. This will secure their confidence in you and your organization.

Follow up methodically. If you don't close, maintain a reasonable follow-up process with very little pressure. Tell them when you are going to call again and why you are calling. For example: "Just want to follow up and see if you need additional information or have any more questions. I'll give you a call back next Thursday the 22nd."

For today write a few of the statements you would ask and strategies you could use for your product or service from each of the steps listed. Identify a prospect with a Compliant behavioral style and use these techniques as soon as possible. Remember, practice makes permanent!

DAY 66
Closing Techniques for
the Influencer/Expressive

Today we will cover how to close the Influencer/Expressive behavioral style. The Influencer's style can pose a problem because of the positive, friendly environment they create. The salesperson who desires to be "liked" does not want to introduce the confrontation of closing into this positive, friendly environment for fear of being disliked. However, there are several ways to approach the Influencer and achieve your goal of closing the sale and remaining a trusted sales professional.

Reinforce their positive comments. Whenever the Influencer makes a positive comment about a feature, benefit, or advantage of your product or service, make sure to reinforce his or her insight. Reinforcing statements such as "That makes a lot of sense" or "I see what you're saying" will keep their optimism high and move them toward the close.

Offer a good deal. The Influencer is often prompted to say "yes" when he/she feels like a good deal is on the table. They are frequently optimistic about your product and trusting of you and what you say about your product. Their tipping point might be the good deal you are offering them today. Keep the good deal in your pocket until you are ready to close.

Close abruptly. A sales call with the Influencer is typically a lot of fun. There's a lot of personal discussion, optimism, and enthusiasm, while making a commitment is not their primary concern. By abruptly closing with a statement like "So, are you ready to move on this?" or "So, do you want to place the order?" puts a temporary damper on the otherwise enjoyable discussion. The Influencer's desire to return to the enjoyable discussion typically gets him or her to answer in the affirmative. If they are not ready to go, they will typically raise a key objection and then you can decide how to deal with the new objection. However, once you address the objection, go right back with another abrupt close.

Watch out for buyer's remorse. Of all the different behavioral styles, the Influencer is the most likely to jump now and think later. As a result you will want to make sure you have them obligated beyond just their written confirmation. Having them authorize your paperwork and providing a down payment are two ways to ensure follow-through. Then, follow up in writing (e-mail, text message, letter, etc.), confirming the good decision they made and the positive "experience" they are about to enjoy.

Provide details, details, details. If you did not give them the detailed information as a "take-away" during or following the sale, then make sure to get it in their hands as soon as possible. If there is another party involved with the purchase and the prospect did not give you that information, you must be prepared that that person may not have an Influencer behavioral style. The other party may want to see the detailed information. When the other party who wants to see details begins to question the Influencer, the sale may be put on hold, or worse, cancelled. By providing the detailed information as a follow-up and calling the Influencer's attention to the fact that you've given them the information "in case someone wants to see the particulars," you've decreased the probability of them backing out of the sale.

No sale? Follow up tenaciously. Of the four different behavioral styles, the Influencer is the fastest to forget about your offer and get caught up in something completely different. When the Influencer is interested, you need to close immediately, if at all possible. If you don't close right away, you must follow up often since the trail will go cold. However, they often re-engage the same way they lose interest—fast!

For today, write a few of the statements you could make and strategies you could use for your product or service from each of the steps listed. Identify a prospect with an Influencer behavioral style and use these techniques as soon as possible. Remember, practice makes permanent!

DAY 67
Closing Techniques for
the Dominant/Driver

Today we will cover how to close the Driven/Dominant behavioral style. The prospect with a Driven/Dominant style can pose a challenge. The Driver's competitive and aggressive style may appear confrontational, causing many salespeople to avoid asking for the order and to leave the appointment feeling dejected. However, with the proper approach, the Driven/Dominant behavioral style can be closed quickly.

Offer two to three alternatives. The Driver has a demanding and strong-willed style and will want to control your exchange. By offering them only one option they are not able to control as much, because they are going along with what you've proposed. They may say "no" simply because they don't feel like they are making a good decision or that they don't like having just one option. If they have more than one option they get to make an informed decision, get to choose, and are more in control. Too many options can be just as counterproductive as a single option, so limit your options to two or three.

They must "win." The competitive nature of Drivers demands they win. This means you should be prepared to negotiate in the event they drive for a concession.

Ask their opinion. Drivers are often egocentric, meaning what they say matters most. As a result you can use questions like "What way do you think is best?" when comparing the two to three options in your proposal. If you ask questions such as "Do you like this?" you are rolling the dice and the odds are not with you. Drivers like to control and may say "no" just because they believe you are trying to direct them.

Only offer suggestions when they ask. Drivers are often pioneering and venturesome, meaning they like to think outside the box. At the same time, they want to control the exchange, and the direction should ultimately come from their ideas. They are prone to ask bigger questions aimed at pushing the envelope, so be cautious with suggestions. When they ask for suggestions, it is a positive sign. Finally, be careful to *only* offer ideas and suggestions that are currently available. If you share some "blue sky" thinking, they may want to wait for the new improved idea you shared.

Close faster than normal and get out. "Be quick, be smart, be gone" may well be the motto when dealing with the Driver. Their demanding, aggressive, and direct style often causes the salesperson to back off in order to avoid what feels like a confrontation. This is a mistake. Their style can mean a faster than normal close.

Ask for their direction. The Driver is often decisive and will move the sale forward if you just ask the question "What's the next step?" If the response is negative, then you clearly know where you stand and you know it sooner rather than later.

Ask for their leadership. Ask "What would you like me to do?" or "What would you like me to do next?" Either of these questions asks them to lead you in the direction you should go. Also, their answers may position you to obtain an obligation from them. It may be appropriate after they answer the question to confirm,

"So, if I am able to get you XYZ, then what's the next step after that?" Occasionally their next statement will be a clear direction and obligation on how to move the sale forward.

For today, write a few of the statements you would ask and strategies you could use because you feel invincible. When you walk, your shoulders are broad and you feel that any prospect who crosses your path will become a customer. Wouldn't this be great if we felt this way all year long?

DAY 68
Dealing with the Initial Objections and Conditions

An objection is a statement by your prospect that he/she wants to know more. Objections are just a front that prospects need more information. Prospects usually object with sincerity, but they don't know any better. The professional salesperson knows this and knows how to handle it. Learn these methods and you will avoid challenge No. 12 from Day 3: failing to handle objections in a proper manner.

Objections are your friends; without them you can't get near the close. You need prospects to be thinking and to get involved. Sometimes prospects already know the answer to the objection and want to see how you answer it. This is called trapping. The prospect may have experience with your product or service. Make sure you have the correct answer, and, in the event you don't, say you will get the answer and get back with him. Do not bluff through the answer because you will lose all credibility, and the prospect won't believe anything you say from there on out. If you need an immediate answer, pick up your cell phone and call immediately, so it does not interfere with your chances of closing.

There are two types of objections: major and minor. Prospects use them to slow things down. This doesn't mean they don't want to buy; they just want to mull things over before committing themselves. Sometimes a prospect will shoot you minor objections just to catch his/her breath or make sure that you can answer his/her minor objections eloquently before things get any farther. Not all problems are objections that can and should be overcome.

You often encounter conditions that prevent the purchase. One huge condition would be that the prospect does not have enough money or credit for a large purchase. This is why prequalifying the lead is vital. True **In-home** sales professionals do not waste time on nonqualified leads or prospects. Maybe the prospect doesn't own the property or home yet and might be in the budgeting stages. A condition is a valid reason for not going ahead. It's not an objection to overcome; it's a total roadblock to the sale, and you must accept it and walk away.

Understand this: Potential buyers who object really cannot see how your offerings will suit their needs. Your job is to use your superior knowledge of what you're selling to show them how it can satisfy their needs. Build Value!

Two Don'ts / One Do

Don't argue. If the prospect needs more information, provide it; don't argue. With anger or sarcasm, or other forms of sales-killing heat and pressure, the salesperson tries to beat the prospect down. Often the salesperson wins the argument and loses all chance of making the sale.

Don't attack your prospects when you overcome their objection. Put space between your prospects and their objections. Develop sensitivity to how your prospects feel when they voice their objections. Never allow prospects to feel that they are in danger of being proven wrong. If you start fighting their feelings, their negative emotions will always take over.

Do lead them to answer their own objections. An **In-home** sales professional always tries to maneuver prospects into answering their own objections because *when they say something, it's true.* Most prospects will answer their own objections if you just work at it, give them time, and lead them to it. Deep down they want to go ahead and purchase; just show them how and guide them.

Some would say that a "no" may mean "not now." However, "maybe" is the one to focus on. This is what you need to master. Much like any famous artist will use every stroke of the paint brush to finish the masterpiece, **In-home** sales professionals will use their skills and techniques to overcome the "maybe."

Stay in form! It is essential that your prospect does not pick up on the fact you are trying to close them. Once the prospect feels you are pushing hard, they will resist you even more. Slow down and try to reduce the amount of pressure. Commit in your mind to staying there a bit longer and investing a little more time, as that small investment of additional time may be the difference between getting the sale or leaving with nothing to show for your initial investment in time.

Remember, "people love to buy, they hate to be sold!" Most of your sales will come after three to five objections. Stay in form and continue to move the sale forward. We will cover all the details on how to handle every objection on Days 71-73.

DAY 69
In-home Sales Mantra No. 19:
Speak and Dress for Success
365 Days a Year

How you speak and carry yourself will dictate how people perceive you. I routinely drive 30,000 miles a year as an **In-home** sales pro. This exposes me to a lot of poor drivers who cut me off, turn in front of me, or just plain break the rules at my expense. My initial reaction was to lash out in rage, and I have had to make major changes with the way I approach these situations. I have put notes on my mirror to "slow down" and kill the hate with love. Now I just wave with a smile. They were expecting a negative stimulus—an inappropriate gesture or an angry word—and you instead gave them a positive stimulus— a wave and a smile. Who knows, this may be a prospect next week! Remember, the person who loses his/her temper loses control, and the **In-home** sales pro always want to be in control.

The second piece is how you carry yourself. At Sales Octane we try as much as possible to look and dress comfortable in casual business attire. You never know who you're going to run into at the supermarket, your kid's soccer game, a church event, or even at a local restaurant while out for lunch. The one time you cheat by tossing on the poor clothes as you head off to the kid's soccer game, you will run into a prospect and you'd like to crawl into a hole. He will mention he is looking for the product or service you provide, and you're saying in your head, "Oh boy, what's my first impression now?" You may get around this by apologizing for being caught off guard but you are still working from a hole you dug for yourself.

If you dress and talk like you are planning to see a prospect, life will get better faster. For today, think about the changes you need to make with the way you speak and carry yourself. It's worth the change!

DAY 70
In-home Sales Mantra No. 20:
Selling from the Heart

I have personally been on a coaching assignment for a large company that has offices in 22 states. In one area of the country they have a serious competitor that offers products at a price point that is 25 to 40 percent lower than their price. When I initially began working with many of the salespeople from this region they were already feeling beaten mentally before the appointment. When they arrive and the prospect mentions he/she is also getting bids from the competitor, some of these salespeople would fold like an accordion.

After running numerous leads and getting beat up, they were feeling that their company and product were not worthy of the 25 to 40 percent higher price, and in a short time their sales hit rock bottom. They had forgotten about selling themselves and all of the features and benefits their company and their product offered to the prospect. They actually stopped believing in their products and their company. Once you stop believing, the prospect will see it and before long you are out of business. You could actually see it in the salesperson's face as he/she knocked on the door. He or she would conduct a horrible needs analysis and would fail to even ask the prospect why he/she was considering the competitor's product.

After seeing this happen several times I focused on the following three points with each of them:

1. You must believe that the company you represent is superior over every other competitor. You must be prepared to prove it, and you must be proud that you represent your company and your product. If you can't believe, aren't prepared, or are not proud, then get another job.

2. You must feel you are underpriced in the marketplace. Yes, I said underpriced even when the competitor's price was 25 to 40 percent below our price. You must believe that your superior product, valuable services, and everything your company offers should actually be higher priced. But to be competitive, your company has chosen this affordable and fair pricing structure. You are presenting the prospect with the opportunity to purchase a superior product at a reasonable price. If you don't believe this in your heart, then get another job.

3. You must believe that you are so good at what you do that you could work for any of your competitors. I said "could work for your competitors," but you chose instead to work for your company because of its superior product, valuable services, and reasonable price, If you don't believe in yourself and your decision to work for a great company, then find another job.

In several months we turned the situation around and began to win more than any previous time in the past. Selling comes from the heart! For today review these three points and see where you need to change your heart.

DAY 71
Address All Possible Objections Early

In-home sales is not a be-back type business. If it were, I would not be writing this book. Once the price is out, either you close your sale and get your prospects happily involved in your product or you're in jeopardy of the next sales rep coming in behind you and closing the sale.

One major key point I want to bring out is that any **In-home** sales professional selling a product/service will address very early all objections he/she may face throughout the sales process. If I know that my product or service is higher priced than my top competitors, I will gradually explain and prepare the prospect. I will say many times, "We will probably be higher, but here is why." Benefits and value. "You see our company is higher because we choose to be. We decided that we wanted to go with the best-trained labor force to install your product as well as bringing the highest quality of material. If we were to reduce the quality of our labor and material, we certainly would be much cheaper."

The choice is yours. Early in the selling cycle I use a disarming statement (see Step 3, Day 39). Here is an example: "John, in a few moments I would like to tell you about my company and product. At any given time if you feel that my product or service, colors, or options do not fit your needs, I will be on my way. I can take a 'no' as well as a 'yes.'" I might mention this somewhere in the warm-up stage. "You may not qualify to be my customer. If you're all about price then I might not be the company for you. At XYZ Decking our service and product that we offer is price competitive for the value and service we bring to the customer. But we certainly won't be the cheapest in the market; we choose not to be." I believe that the key to success is not how many people you see or talk to; it's about how many *qualified* prospects you talk to on a daily/weekly basis.

When you're in sales and striving to be the best, understand a few key points about price. If people were all about price, why would people:

- Drive a Mercedes when a Ford Focus does the exact same thing?

- Live in a $1 million home when you can live modestly in a $100,000 home?

- Wear $200 shoes when many discount stores have shoes for $40 or less?

- Wear an $8,000 Rolex watch when you can find $75 watches all day long?

- Put their kids in private schools when their taxes already pay for public schools?

- Wear designer clothes when there are many discount clothing options available?

- Use cable or Dish TV when many local channels are available for free?

- Pay $5 for a coffee drink when there are many options for a $1 cup of coffee?

The point is, people will pay if they feel they are getting the value for the dollar spent.

DAY 72
Five Steps for
Overcoming Objections

Now is a perfect time to address objections. Here are five steps for handling objections:

1. Use a softening statement after you hear your prospect out completely. For example:

- "I completely understand how you feel."

- "Some of my best customers felt that way also."

- "That's not the first time I heard that in my career."

2. Isolate and question the objection. For example:

Prospect: "The price is too high."

In-home sales pro: "I understand. Let me ask you a question. Assuming the price on this deck wasn't an issue, or it did fit within your budget—maybe even someone was going to purchase it for you—is it the right solution for your needs today?"

3. Let the prospect answer the objection. Once you uncover the real objection, answer it.

4. Confirm that you answered their question/objection. Don't talk past your close, because it might introduce more objec-

tions. Just use a scripted response and confirm their answer. For example:

- "Does that answer your question?"

- "Does that make sense?"

- "Does that satisfy your concern?"

5. Ask for the order (this could be your second or fifth attempt). Ask again and shut up!

For suggestions on additional ways to close, see Appendix A-1 through A-5.

DAY 73
In-home Objections
and Your Responses

Here are some of my favorite objections and our suggested responses:

Objection! "We need to think about it."

In-home sales pro response: "You know, John, I understand. I know I have given you a lot of information, and some customers I speak with tell me the same thing. Before I take off, I'm concerned that I may have stressed the _____(use a part of your presentation) a little too much, What do you think?"

Objection! "I never make decisions on the first visit."

This should have been caught in Step 7, the trial close.

Objection! "I have another bid coming in two days."

This information could have been found in Step 3, warm up, and also in Step 4 Visual Inspection.

Objection! "I need to talk to my spouse."

This is a one-leg appointment and could have been caught in Step 2. Try to reduce this by getting all the decision makers present for the appointment. Without all the decision makers present, there is a high probability you will get this objection. In the event you do, here is a sample script you can you use.

In-home sales pro: "I understand that. Let me ask you a question before I leave. If your spouse said to you, 'I'm fine with whatever you decide,' what would be your decision right now?"

Objection! "It's more than we can afford."

This is an easy one because if you isolate this as the real objection, then you can handle it. The first thing is, if you built the dream in the design step (Step 8), you can use the take-away close (Appendix A6). You must find the real number they can afford, and by now you should have a decent budget number. For example:

In-home sales pro: "So, John, I came in a bit more than you were expecting. I mean, I'm at $19,250. Did you think it was going to be around $19,000 even?" (Stop and shut up, also stay close to your figure. That way you don't give them a huge spread to choose from.)

Prospect "Well, no, we figured it for around $18,000."

In-home sales pro: "Great, we are not that far apart. Was $18,000 based on anything factual, like a newspaper ad or another bid?"

Prospect: "Yes, another bid."

In-home sales pro: "Perfect, I'm guessing that my material and craftsmanship is where the difference is, but let's first make sure the product and design are similar. Please grab that bid and let me confirm."

If they show the bid to you, you're 95 percent home. If they don't, the objection was a smokescreen or a stall. If the bid's product or design is very close to yours, then say, "I see we are close. If you had to choose between companies, if they were the same price, you mostly would go with me, wouldn't you?"

Prospect: "Yes, you're a much better company"

In-home sales pro: "So you see why I'm $1,250 higher?"

Prospect: "Yes I do; better company, better installation crews, and better product."

In-home sales pro: "Thanks I appreciate that. So, basically, all you need to think about is the $1,250 difference?"

Prospect: "Pretty much, it's a lot of money to me".

At this point use the take away close (Appendix A-6) and get the prospect back in the budget area. See if you can take away something in the $1,250 range. If they want the building just as it is, use the reduce to pennies close (Appendix A-3) and reduce the $1,250 into cents a day over a period of time.

Always try to convert every objection to "We need to think about it," and then find out if the objection is a stall or put off.

DAY 74
Following Up with the Dominant/Driver

There are specific follow-up steps to use based on the behavioral style of your prospect, which you identified on Day 16. Follow these steps for the Dominant/Driver:

- Follow up as promised. Drivers are very result oriented and keep their commitments. They expect others to do the same. Whatever you commit to doing for a Driver, make sure you meet or exceed that commitment in the time frame promised.

- Give them credit. When you follow up with Drivers, it's a good strategy to give them credit for anything they pointed out or clarified during or since the call.

- Manage their expectations. Be detailed with what they should expect from you along with specific time frames.

- Continue to mention credible references. Drivers are egocentric and like to be associated with other important individuals. Reference anyone they may find impressive in your correspondence.

- Nurture with knowledge. Drivers like to be in the know so constantly send information they may find useful. This keeps your name in front of them while providing them with valuable information.

- Expand your reach. Sometimes Drivers are so focused on another result that they put your issue on hold. If you are not getting a response, evaluate working with others who are significant to your contact.

Review this list whenever you are following up after an appointment. Knowing how to best approach prospects based on their behavioral style may be the edge you need to get the return call.

DAY 75
Following up with
the Influencer/Expressive

Specific follow-up steps to use based on the Influencer/Expressive behavioral style of your prospect, which you identified on . If your prospect or customer is an Influence then:

- Follow up often. Influencers tend to over-commit which means they may have other new issues that put your issue out of sight and mind. By following up often, you increase the probability they will re-engage with you.

- Come up with something personal to include with your follow-up. Whatever their interest (sports, family, leisure, etc.), they will be more inclined to connect with you if it's not all business.

- Follow up with the rest of the information. If you did not give them the detailed information as a take-away from your appointment, this makes a great reason to follow up. Get the detailed information in their hands fast, especially if others are involved in the decision-making process (who are Drivers, Steadys or Compliants).

- Use a take-away. If appropriate, reinforce what they might miss if they wait too long. This may be just the push they need to get them over the edge and return your call.

Review this list whenever you are following up after an appointment with the Influencer. Knowing how to best approach prospects based on their behavioral style may be the edge you need to get the return call.

DAY 76
In-home Sales Mantra No. 21:
Leverage Your Longevity,
or When Bigger May Be Better

Here's a test to take: Cut out the Yellow Pages section of your phone book or make a copy of all the listings under the heading "Construction" or "Contractors." Come back to that same page one year later and you will find that 50 percent of the phone numbers are disconnected; come back five years later and 90 percent of the phone numbers will be disconnected.

In today's economy people get laid off from their jobs, and the following week they are **In-home** contractors. They may or may not do a good job on the initial work but here is the big question: Where will they be when they go back to their big-paying job with benefits? I have a relative that has been through at least 15 strikes while working for a large company. During the strikes he became a painter, deck builder, and handyman to feed his family. When he gets called back to work, there will not be customer service or follow-up for his previous customers.

For today, make a list of all the things your company has to offer that separates you from the fly-by-night operation. You are committed to the **In-home** business as a specialist and you need to separate yourself from the competition.

DAY 77
In-home Sales Mantra No. 22:
Be Genuine and Positive

This is a perfect time to talk about being genuine and positive. Imagine if all the prospects you met on a weekly basis were sincere, authentic and honest. They would answer honestly, share their issues freely and take real interest in whatever you said. Better yet, what would happen if you were to demonstrate your product/service with these same character traits? The answer is your sales would sky rocket. People buy from people they like and people buy from people that are similar to themselves. When you arrive for your appointment there is a good possibility that the sales representative from your competitor came in before you and did not demonstrate these character traits. Even though their price might have been lower you will get the sale. The prospect will sense how genuine you are about your product and service and this fills the value gap and gets them moving forward with investing in your product or service.

Second is the issue of being positive. By pairing yourself with positive comments and positive people you separate yourself from the competition. Customers would much rather be surrounded by others who look at the glass half full. Customers would rather hear from a salesperson who is focused on the positive and not the negative. Remember, whatever you pair yourself with you become!

Not only are customers attracted to a positive sales professional but you will also improve. By removing negative thoughts and comments and focusing on the positive you have paired yourself with the very things you want to embrace; possibility and potential.

For today, listen to the comments that come out of your mouth. Focus on what you are thinking about and pouring into your mind. Look at who you surround yourself with throughout the day. Then make sure you are genuine and positive as you strive to become an In-home Sales Professional!

DAY 78
Following Up with
the Steady/Amiable

Specific follow-up steps to use based on the Steady/Amiable behavioral style of your prospect, which you identified on Day 16 are the following:

- Come up with something personal to include with your follow-up. Whatever their interest (sports, family, leisure, etc.), they will be more inclined to connect with you if it's not all business.

- Don't push. Maintain a reasonable follow-up process with a little pressure, especially if they have told you they have a pressing date/issue. Steadys are very patient and expect others to act in a similar patient manner.

- Create a tipping point. Making them aware of an upcoming price increase, change in the product line, or lead time extension are reasons that might get them to return your call. However, do not pressure them as that will backfire.

- Offer bargains. Steadys like a bargain, so if you have a "new limited" offer you can use this to re-engage.

- Minimize their risk. Continue to follow up with references of others who are succeeding with your product/service. This makes them feel better about investing with you.

Review this list whenever you are following up after an appointment. Knowing how to best approach prospects based on their behavioral style may be the edge you need to get the return call.

DAY 79
Following Up with
the Compliant/Analytical

Specific follow-up steps to use based on the Compliant/Analytical behavioral style of your prospect, which you identified on Day 16 are the following:

- Manage the expectations. Be detailed with what they should expect from you along with specific time frames. If something changes with the time frame, immediately make them aware of the changes.

- Don't push. Maintain a reasonable follow-up process with very little pressure. Compliants are very methodical when making a decision so plan for a longer response time than with a Driver or Influencer.

- Create a tipping point. Making them aware of an upcoming price increase, change in the product line, or lead time extension are reasons that might get them to return your call. However, do not pressure them as that will backfire.

- Send additional information. Mail them something that can supplement the materials you gave them initially. Use that as a follow-up to make sure they received it and to answer any questions they may have.

Review this list whenever you are following up after an appointment. Knowing how to best approach prospects based on their behavioral style may be the edge you need to get the return call.

DAY 80
You Won! Reward Yourself

Stop for today. If you have followed our instructions, you have read one day each of the last 80 days. You've been very busy learning and practicing several new techniques and also sharpening your skills with ideas from this book—skills that you have already acquired from your previous selling experience. Too often we get so busy selling that we miss the opportunity to pat ourselves on the back for a job well done.

Years ago I learned that having goals was vital to my sales success. Someone also taught me to reward myself when I achieve the goals. This is based on the concept that whatever you reinforce you get more of. If I reinforce my wife for a great meal she has cooked, she is more likely to make more of those great meals. If I reinforce my children when they get good grades, clean their rooms, or make good decisions, they are more likely to continue to get good grades, keep their rooms clean, and make good decisions. Whatever I reinforce tends to occur more often in the future.

So why do we not reinforce ourselves? Why do we not stop and pat ourselves on the back when we get a sale? Why do we not reward ourselves when we hit a major goal such as a sales quota? The reason is simple: We just don't think about it.

Take a minute today and be thankful for the sale you just made. Reinforce yourself! Then take a look at your goals and identify one major goal that you want to accomplish. When you accomplish that goal, how are you going to reward yourself? Is it going to be a day off? Dinner with your spouse, significant other, or friend? Perhaps you should hold off on that purchase you want to make and have that as your reward.

Once you know how you are going to reward yourself for that next major goal, we want you to accumulate some pictures of that reward. Look at those pictures often as you go about your day. It will drive you to work smarter and push toward your goal. And when you achieve your goal, you will reward yourself and that will reinforce you. Whatever you reinforce you get more of. It's the cycle of success that is guaranteed with the 10 Step **In-home** Sales **Continuum**™.

When you reach a goal using the techniques from the *First 100 Days of In-home Selling,* please contact us and share the experience. Send us a photo of how you rewarded yourself by going to www.salesoctane.com and selecting the Contact Us link.

DAY 81
A Quick Word on Paperwork

The reason why we made paperwork an actual step in the 10 Step **In-home** Sales **Continuum**™ is because back when I was in my prime—a closing machine—I had horrible paperwork. I have probably trained, hired, and coached well over 5,000 salespeople and over the years, I noticed a small trend. Most salespeople are out for the victory of the sale and hurry the paperwork process. They tend to be a bit lazy on paperwork. Some are new to their careers and, when they get to the paperwork part, they look at it and go, oh boy, now what do I do?

Companies should require a thorough drawing that is detailed, and error free because it's a legal document. Go home or to your office after the sale and complete a full detailed agreement without hesitations. We need to end bad sloppy paperwork right here. Incomplete paperwork also makes the people you work with and who process your documents view you differently. If you make their job difficult and they always have to chase you to get change orders, you may fall out of favor with them.

In most companies, one third of your job is to make the sale, one third is proper paperwork with no change orders, and the last third is get the product manufactured, delivered, and built (installed) on time so you can collect the final installment with no problems.

The key component of the paperwork is that it is complete and readable, and the customer gets an installation that is exactly what is written on the legal document. Also know the back side of your legal agreements, so if your customer asks a question you have a professional, honest answer. If there are key points they need to know before signing, have them initial by the key point.

Here is a good example: If your company does not remove the remaining debris from the job site upon completion and the customer is responsible for the removal, make sure the customer knows this upfront so you do not give him/her a surprise at the signing stage. He/she will not get angry after job completion and you will not have friction when trying to collect the final installment. It is best to be upfront from the beginning.

Another good example in today's economy is that certain companies require some sort of bank authorization document, which basically is proof that the funds are available. Customers would rather know about this requirement upfront and not be surprised as you're completing the final documents.

Make sure you have a brochure packet/folder to put their copies of the agreement with your business card inside. Sometimes people might wake up in the middle of the night and review what they have signed. Good penmanship will drastically help in this case; make sure the copies are readable. A good idea is to place an extra business card inside the brochure/agreement package and let the customer know there is an extra one in there.

I firmly believe that customers need to know what they are signing. Please slow down during Step 9 and read the document to them line by line. It works!

DAY 82
Step 10: Thank-you Cards

As we discussed earlier, people buy from people they like. Your business will grow as you get people to like you and refer you to others. And while likeability and trust are different, they have one thing in common. Customers have to like you before they will trust you. Once they like you and you bring them value with your product and service, they may begin to trust you and your company. Once they trust you and your company, they will refer you to other people they know. When you arrive at this point in your selling career, you will begin to see major increases in your income with much less effort.

We begin the referral process with a simple thank-you card. Sit back and think of the last thank-you card you received. Did it make you feel good? What was your impression of the person, regardless of whether you purchased from him/her or not? If you received the card prior to making the decision, did you feel the card added a nice touch?

You should always send out thank-you cards, whether you won or lost the sale.

Here are a few rules to thank-you notes/cards:

- Keep them short and simple. If you don't like to write, then use much the same wording with each card.

- Get to the point. Have two to three well-thought-out statements that you routinely include in your cards and make sure your statements are to the point.

- Make them quick. One of the biggest challenges to writing a note is the process of getting your thoughts down on paper. If you are using several statements routinely, then this process will go quickly. If you try to write a new idea in every card, you will give up and stop doing this valuable step.

- Write it personally. Use the first name of your customer(s) and, if appropriate, reference something personal as a "p.s."

- Be specific. The statements you use should include something about the customer's project, situation, or world.

Here is a sample greeting when you won the sale:

Bob and Marsha,

I want to thank you for the opportunity to help you with your new (area where your product/service was used). I enjoyed working with the two of you and look forward to helping you again in the future.

Sincerely,

Ron

P.S. Go Spartans!!

Sample greeting when you lost the sale:

Bob and Marsha,

I want to thank you for the opportunity to work with you on your new (area where your product/service was

used). I enjoyed working with the two of you and if you ever need my services again please don't hesitate to call.
Sincerely,
Ron
P.S. Go Spartans!!

As you will notice, the lines are much the same between winning and losing a sale. The key is that when you send a thank-you note to a prospect who went with your competitor or chose to do nothing on the project, you leave the door open for their next project. If you don't send a thank-you note, then prospects will never call you when they run into problems with your competitor!

Other Times When Sending a Card Is Helpful

After you've made a telephone contact with a hard-to-reach prospect:

> I look forward to meeting with you next (day/date/time). Our company feels quality as well as excellent service is the foundation for any successful business. I look forward to demonstrating for you our great quality products and excellent service.

After a demonstration/presentation that has not yet been closed:

> Thank you for giving me the great opportunity to discuss our product and service with you. Our company feels quality as well as excellent service is the foundation for any successful business. I will call you next (day/date) to follow up.

After receiving a referral from a customer/prospect:

> Thank you for the kind referral. My goal is to provide a professional and quality product for the Wilsons. Rest assured they will receive the highest level of professionalism and service from me.

Another line you can use after you have won the sale:

> Thank you for the opportunity to provide you with the finest product and service in the marketplace. I feel confident you will be happy with this investment. My goal is to make sure your job runs smooth and we meet all your expectations. Another goal is excellent follow-up service so you will some day refer me to others who may have needs similar to yours.

Your company may already have thank-you cards, or you may have to purchase them yourself. Personalizing your thank-you cards with your name is a nice touch. However, preprinted canned thank-you notes like the ones you get from a vendor on your birthday will not impress anyone. You have to write them and also write the mailing information on the envelope. That shows you are interested in making a positive impression. When I receive a card that is handwritten, I get the feeling this person really cares by taking time out of their day for me.

Make a goal to send out at least two to five cards per day. If you are just getting started, then send cards to contractors and agents in order to generate some interest.

In-home Sales Pro Tip:: **In-home** sales professionals carry a roll of stamps and thank-you cards/envelopes in their briefcases so they can write the notes and put them in the mail as soon after the meeting as possible. If you wait too long, you will forget. Days turn to weeks and weeks turn to never. Put these items on your packing list for your briefcase and make it happen.

DAY 83
In-home Sales Mantra No. 23:
No Sales, No Earnings
Equal No Fun

You can be smart, appealing, a smooth talker, and even a great presenter, but if you can't close a sale you won't earn any money and you won't have any fun. I have learned that no matter where I travel or what state I am in, prospects can still be closed on the first visit. If you think they won't or can't make a decision to say "yes" on your first visit, you are already behind in the sale.

Everything you do and say and how you act should be guided toward closing the sale on the first appointment. The ultimate reward is when they sign that written agreement and hand you the check. This is what the **In-home** sales pro works for on every call. Your creed should always be: "I lead and guide prospects into making a decision that is right for them, and I create urgency to make that happen."

Over the years we have had numerous salespeople come to our Sales Octane training workshops and endlessly try to explain to us that people in their state or city cannot be closed on the first appointment. And, every time, we return months later to find that person is no longer working at the company. They have taken a position that requires them to simply ask the question: "Would you like to supersize that?" These salespeople allow fear and excuses to create their own roadblocks that prevent them from closing on the first appointment.

In order to become an **In-home** sales pro you must have the ability, desire, and willingness to close the sale on your first appointment. Closing is an art and skill, and it is the craft of the **In-home** sales pro. The **In-home** sales pro understands he or she needs to make at least five attempts to close the sale on the first visit. These attempts take timing and skill. Hang in there, practice your skills and techniques in this book, and before long you will master the art of closing.

For today, write a list of all the reasons why selling and closing sales are important to you. What makes you tick and gets you motivated? Compare this list to your written goals from Day 4 and Do not give up!

DAY 84
In-home Sales Mantra No. 24: Creating Real Value Is Not Just About the Product or Service You Sell

"Creating value" is a buzzword that typically focuses on the benefits your customers experience when they use your product or service. When we say creating value we go beyond the benefits a customer experiences with the use of your product and service.

Creating real value can be the positive effect you have on others. It can be your smile or the thank-you note you send. It is the way you greet people and the way you reinforce them honestly and sincerely. It is the extra mile you go for others. Creating real value is anything you do for another person that helps them. You can never create too much value. Work hard, work with integrity, and create real value, and your success is assured.

For today, list 10 reasons why people should buy from you and review the list daily!

DAY 85
Preparing to Turn Satisfied
Customers into Numerous Referrals

Experience shows referrals have a much greater chance of closing and take less time to close than a non-referred lead. Most **In-home** sales companies expect you to keep improving your closing ratio. For instance, if your company gives you 10 leads a week and they expect a 30 percent closing percentage, then if you exceed that percentage you secure your income and your position at the company. During the next three days we will cover the science behind how to get more referrals to improve your closing ratio.

The best time to get the referral is at the final installment. When you first began the sales process you entered into a written agreement and collected an initial installment to execute the agreement. Most companies have a final installment at the end of the process, and it's at this point you get the customer to confirm that you and your company did what you said you would do.

After you have received the final payment, this is a perfect time to ask for names and numbers of other people they know who might need your product or service. You should expect to get referrals after you have provided value to your customer by meeting all of their expectations. If you did all the things you said you would do and your company did a great job on the project, why would they not want to refer you to others? Here's the process:

During or right after the final appointment to collect the final installment, you say: "Mr. Jones, let me ask you a question. We started this process six weeks ago and I want to make sure I have met your expectations."

Customer: "Ron you did a great job and we are very, very happy."

In-home sales pro: "Mr. Jones, that's great. Thanks again for letting me help you out. You know, this is how I make my living, making people happy and getting them happily involved with my product. Who can you think of that might also need this product/ service?"

Don't be surprised when they say "Ron, right now I can't think of anyone, but if I do I will be sure to give them one of your cards. Why don't you give me a dozen or so cards?"

The reality is that you might as well give them a box of kindling wood because that's what your dozen cards will be used for. The only reason they asked for your cards is because they felt obligated because you reminded them of the great job you did and they feel bad they could not come up with a name. The reason that customers have such a difficult time thinking of possible referrals is twofold. First, they are not sure what you're looking for, and, second, your request is too broad and they can't picture the faces of their friends, neighbors, or colleagues who may be ideal referrals. To help them see the faces of potential referrals, you want to do two things:

1. *Hand them the View-Master®.* When I was younger, one of my favorite toys was the View-Master®. I would put one of those circular cards in with several pictures/images of animals or

cartoon characters. When I clicked through the images, I could see all of these different pictures. The brain of your customer works much the same way. You need to help them see prospective referrals. To do that you need to figure out which groups (such as sports or hobby), associations, church, and non-profits they belong to. We refer to these groups as the "circles they run in." From the moment you arrive at their home, you need to be looking for evidence of what circles they run in. It may be a bumper sticker or a decal on their car or truck. It may be something that hangs on the wall or their refrigerator. It may be the logo on a jacket or shirt. At the very least we know that one of their circles is their neighborhood and their place of employment.

2. *Give them a condition.* Once you know a circle your customer runs in, you then want to give your customer a condition or two for when a prospective customer would need your

product or service. For instance, if you sell replacement windows, then one of the conditions for someone needing your product is when that person moves into a home or when someone is renovating a home. Another condition could be when someone buys and owns rental property or flips/renovates homes.

For today, write down how you can identify the customer's circles and the conditions when someone would need your product or service. Tomorrow we will show you how you combine these two in an effort to secure numerous referrals.

DAY 86
Helping Them "See" Referrals for You

Now that you've told your customers how you build your business with referrals and you've confirmed with them that you went above and beyond to make them satisfied customers, it's time to hand them the View-Master® and talk them through the process of giving you referrals.

Simply take the first circle they run in and then combine it with a couple of conditions. (Note: Do not throw out two to three circles at the same time. That would be like shoving three of those discs into your View-Master®, and all you would see is a bunch of nothing. Go with one circle at a time.) Here's how it works.

The customer just finished saying, "Ron, right now I can't think of anyone, but if I do I will be sure to give them one of your cards. Why don't you give me a dozen or so cards?"

In-home sales pro: "No problem, I can certainly leave you some cards. Hey, let me ask you a question. When we first met you told me you were a member of 4-H. Oftentimes people who have moved recently or are renovating their home need my services. Who can you think of in 4-H that moved or is renovating their home?" Bang! They are seeing the faces of the folks at their last 4-H gathering, and now you just continue to prime them with conditions.

In-home sales pro: "...Or people who either own rental property or renovate and flip property also really benefit from what I
do. Who in 4-H has rental property?"

Then go to the next circle they run in and use the same conditions. You may also want to suggest that customers grab their
personal phone directories or 4-H telephone directories in case
that might help. By continuing to share with you the groups, orga-
nizations, and "circles they run in" as well as the names of anyone
in those groups who might need your product or service, you are
assured three to five names. These names are fuel for your 10
Step **In-home** Sales **Continuum™**.

What if you had an issue during the installation or implementation of the project? Even if you have had a snag, by handling the
repair or problem immediately, you will find that you build more
value with customers. Whenever customers call with an issue, you
must respond as soon as possible. No one wants to enter into an
agreement and have the sales rep vanish. If this happens, you can
throw away your credibility and your referrals. Remember that in
your meet-and-greet stage (Step 3), you found out what they do
for a living or any hobbies, clubs, and associations they belong to.
Remember, the cycle does not stop after a sale. You must get at
least three to five referrals. Referrals will keep you in a forward
motion to make more sales and more money.

Leave extra business cards or a gift with your card. For example,
you just installed a $50,000 kitchen for the Johnsons and they had
a holiday party to show off their new investment to family and
friends. Of course, Mary or Martha saw this new kitchen and said,
"Wow, breathtaking. Who did this job for you?" At this point the
Johnsons will say "XYZ Kitchens, and the rep was just awesome.
He met all our needs." And the Johnsons will hand over to Mary
and Martha one of the extra business cards you left them.

DAY 87
Getting Your Customer to Refer You

After your customer can't "see" any additional referrals, thank them for the names and then ask them for all the details:

- Make sure you have the correct spelling of the referral's name.

- Get the referral's contact information, telephone number, e-mail, etc.

- If your customer has not already told you why he/she thought of the referral, ask, "Why did you think of Bob Jones?" This will be helpful information and provide the "reason" you will use when you make your prospecting call to Bob Jones.

- Ask your customers if they would be willing to make a call to the referral to introduce you. For example, "Gail, would you be willing to make an introduction for me to Bob?" If they are unwilling to make an introduction, usually because they are not that close with the person, then make sure you ask them to suggest the next step.

- Ask if you can use the customer's name as a reference. For example, "Gail, can I use your name as a reference when I call Bob?" Almost 100 percent of the time they will agree to let you use their name and that's all you really need to create the environment to secure an appointment.

That's it! Now you have a few referrals to put into the **In-home** Sales **Continuum**™, beginning with the material from Day 11.

DAY 88
Rewarding the Referrer

When you give you receive. That's not the reason we should give but the principle still works. When someone gives you a referral, he/she improves your opportunity to sell. Referrals are the secret of sales success. Therefore, you owe the person who gives you a referral.

At the same time, the principle of reinforcement comes into play; whatever you reinforce, you get more of. Because you want others to continue to give you referrals, if you reinforce them with rewards, they are inclined to give you more referrals. Not only do you owe them for the referrals, you want to reward them because it will motivate them to give you additional referrals.

When Should You Reward Them?

You typically reward customers for a referral when the referral has resulted in a sale or after you have been paid. You may bait them with a commitment to "make it worth their while," but you reward them when it becomes a sale. If you reward them when they give you the referral, they are going to expect to be rewarded with each referral regardless of the outcome. When a particular referral does not result in a sale, it's difficult to renegotiate. By waiting to reward them after the sale you keep them engaged during the entire sales process.

Once the sale has been completed or the invoice has been paid in full, you want to be diligent in following through with the reward. Once you set the expectation and begin rewarding people for referrals, you will notice how they often keep track of the sales. If you get busy or, worse, greedy and fail to reward them, you will not only shut off the flow of referrals but also "pair" yourself with a negative ("That salesperson did not follow through!")

What Should You Use as a Reward?

What you use as a reward often becomes a significant point of discussion. The first choice is whether to use money or gifts. Money is only the best option if you know that money will truly motivate them to give you more referrals. Write the check and watch the flow of additional referrals.

The second choice is a gift. What type of gift is important. You want to provide them with gifts that will pass at least two of these three tests:

1. *It's experiential.* Give them something they get to experience. Reward them with a gift card for a dinner to their favorite restaurant. Give them a certificate for a round of golf at a local golf course or maybe a pair of tickets to a ballgame. The key is to give them a reward they will *experience.*

2. *It's emotional.* Reward them with several tickets for their favorite sports team or with sports memorabilia from their hero. Give them something that stirs up emotion and you pair yourself with that positive emotion.

3. *It engages another person (not you).* Picture this: You reward someone with a gift certificate to his/her favorite restaurant. Better yet, you made some calls and found out his/her spouse or significant other's favorite restaurant. Toward the end of dinner, the bill comes, the gift card goes down,

and the other person asks, "Who gave you the gift card?" They answer that it came from a salesperson, which begs the question "Why?" They explain that the gift card was thanks for a referral. The next statement from the other person will be something along the line of "give them *more* referrals!"

Many times during our workshops salespeople will ask whether taking a customer who gave you a referral to lunch or to a sporting event is an appropriate way of rewarding him or her for a referral. Our response is usually "no." If you are there, then it's eventually going to result in a discussion of business and that's not a reward. If you gave your customer two to four tickets or a restaurant gift certificate so he/she could take his/her spouse or significant other/kids/another couple, *and* you're not with your customer, it's a good gift.

How Should You Position the Reward?

Be sure to pair the reward with the reason for the reward. Send a thank-you note and share with the referrer that you appreciated the connection he or she made and that it ultimately resulted in a sale. Thank the referrer for his/her help.

Now you've tied the reward with the reason for the reward and you've made it personal and emotional. Be prepared to receive other referrals.

Two Things to Avoid with Referral Rewards

1. *Don't follow up.* Don't make a call a few days after the sporting event or a few weeks after you sent them the gift certificate to see how they enjoyed their time out. This appears that you are making the call to see if they have other leads. Let it go. When you give you receive. Let the principle work.

2. *Don't stop.* There's a tendency to stop rewarding after a while, especially if you are getting a lot of leads from a particular person. As soon as you stop rewarding, then you are reinforcing that you don't care about leads. Don't forget that without their leads you would not have the sale or the commission in the first place. When you give you receive, so keep giving!

DAY 89
Networking with Agents and Brokers: Link to Their Line

If in your **In-home** business you also work with agents, brokers, or other business interests who refer you to prospects, then you want to use our **LINK** process.

To help you put a structure or process in place for developing relationships with agents, brokers, and other business contacts, we want you to think about the word "link." We developed the **LINK** program to help with your networking efforts. If you think about it, the word "link" is perfect because that's what you're really doing when you go out and network with these potential partners. You link yourself with the person you meet, and you link the person you meet with others in your network. You also try to link them with what you can do for them.

Each letter in the **LINK** program stands for something. It's an acronym for the four types of information needed to engage with someone whom you want to network with over time.

L is for the line of business the person is in. In most cases you already know this because you are intentionally targeting this person because of his/her line. But this goes deeper than just simply the person's title. Imagine you are at a networking venue put on by a local organization, such as the local Chamber of Commerce. You know a few people there but there are many people you've never met. Most **In-home** salespeople head into these engagements with the intent of hanging out with people they know, talking about life, and leaving once they've had their fill of food. Instead the **In-home** sales pro looks for an opportunity to "collide" with someone they have not met. As an **In-home** sales pro, you need four items as you head off to this networking venue: the LINK process, your business cards, your pen, and a burning desire to help someone out with *your* network.

When you engage with someone, simply get them talking. Begin by asking, "So, what brings you here?" and after the person finishes answering your question simply ask, "What do you do?" People love to talk about themselves. Once you identify the person's line, move on to the next step in the link process found in Day 92.

By the way, when you meet someone who is not an agent, broker, or has a direct impact on your business, don't make the mistake of dismissing him or her just because he/she is not a good prospect for your products/services. One of the goals of networking is to grow your network, and *everyone* is a potential link for your network.

DAY 90
In-home Sales Mantra No. 25:
You Give, You Get

As mentioned in Day 84, creating value is more than simply the product or service you sell. When we say "creating value," we mean every opportunity to make a positive impact on everyone you come in contact with.

One of our corporate values at Sales Octane is, "we strive to make a positive contribution to everyone we meet." That is pretty black and white. We do not spend a lot of time trying to define this for our team members or our customers because it is a way of life. It can be your smile or the thank-you note you send. It is the way you greet people, the way you reinforce them honestly and sincerely. It can be the extra mile you go for others. Creating real value is anything you do for other people that helps them.

My neighbor was driving down the road one day and noticed a man riding a bicycle. It was near fall/winter and quite cold out. My neighbor stopped and said, "You look real cold and you have no protection for your hands." Of course, the guy was stunned and replied, "Yes I am very cold."

At that moment my neighbor took off his $40 pair of gloves and said, "You need these gloves more than I do. Here, take these." At this point the man was surprised and thankful as my neighbor drove off. In days to come my neighbor would see the same man riding his bike in the blistering cold and would glance at him and smile as he drove by and noticed the bicyclist was wearing the gloves. My neighbor did not do this for glory or recognition. He did it because it was the right thing to do. When you have this internal compassion for others and act on that compassion, good things happen. When you give, you get. We don't give in order to get, but that's typically the way it works.

You can never create too much value. Work hard, with integrity, create real value, and your success is assured.

> We make a living by what we get,
> We make a life by what we GIVE.
> —Winston Churchill

For today, make a list of items to donate and time you can contribute. Once you find your fit, make this a monthly routine and be charitable. If possible, ask your family to accompany you on your visits.

DAY 91
In-home Sales Mantra No. 26:
The Things That Are Easy to Do
Are Just as Easy Not to Do

There is an old saying, "An apple a day keeps the doctor away." Let's assume for a moment that this statement is 100 percent accurate and *guaranteed*. If you eat one apple every day, it will greatly reduce doctor visits and increase your health and endurance.

Here's the question: How many people would start eating an apple a day? Would you? How long before people would stop eating an apple a day because they were not seeing immediate results? They would miss a few days in a row and before long they would stop altogether. What's the point? It is just as easy not to eat an apple a day as it is to eat an apple a day.

It's easy to stop reading this book at Day 91, even though it's only 10 to 15 minutes a day. We know that, if you read the book your sales results will improve. We know that if you practice the techniques on a daily basis, you will become an expert in a few years. You won't see major changes immediately, but you won't with a correct diet, physical exercise, or anything else that has long-term benefits.

Ask yourself why top professional athletes make so much money. Is it because they were born with the skills or was it because they practiced and persevered? Why does it look so easy for them to sink the putt, put the basketball through the hoop, or the soccer ball in the goal? Why does it look so natural for them to cast that line and hook that bass? The reason why they are great is simple. They practice every day, even when they know it's just as easy not to.

Today, look at your calendar and decide when you will practice every day for the next week. Set aside 10 to 15 minutes a day and put it on your calendar. Identify which steps in the **In-home Sales Continuum™** are your weakest and review those days in this book. Share your calendar with an accountability partner and ask him or her to hold you accountable. Because you know your accountability partner will be asking how you did, you will make the time to practice. At the end of this book, in a little over a week, see if these days don't feel a bit different because you consistently practiced. Do this and you will avoid challenge No. 13 from Day 3: skipping steps or taking short cuts once you're comfortable. It's just as easy to do it as it is not to.

DAY 92
Link to Interests: Find Out
What They Do for Fun

In the **LINK** approach for the four types of information needed to engage with someone whom you want to network with over time, "**I**" is for interests. Once you have information about what line of business the person is in, you want to know what interests he or she has. This may take a few questions like, "Where are you from?" "Have you always lived in this location?" "Are you originally from this area?" One of my favorite questions to get this type of information is, "What do you do for fun?" People love to talk about themselves, and they really like to talk about their passions. So why not ask them about their interests?

When you think about the **LINK** process, visualize a manual merry-go-round at a playground. If you have a few children on the merry-go-round, it takes a fair amount of effort and energy to get it moving. You grab hold of the merry-go-round and start to push it. You dig your feet into the dirt as you run faster and faster and push the merry-go-round harder and harder. Then, once you get it up to speed, you stand off to the side and simply give it a good push every so often to keep it going.

This is how the **LINK** process of questioning works:

• We have to intentionally approach people.

- We have to ask intentional, focused questions to get them talking.

- Once we get them talking, it takes less effort to keep the conversation going and learn about them.

Don't be in a hurry to move beyond the interests conversation. This is where you develop rapport, even though they are typically doing most of the talking. Common areas that come up during the interests conversation include their children, business, sports, coaching, family, travel, and music. The key is to get them talking about themselves and make a mental note of these interests for later.

Don't Push Too Hard

All of this is part of the selling process, but it can't be too obvious. One of the major errors salespeople make is they push too hard and too fast regarding business opportunities. Think about it this way, if you are an **In-home** salesperson, should you really expect a broker or agent to get you some leads the first time you meet? The answer is typically "no." It takes a few weeks, months, and sometimes years to get them to refer or give you leads. Because people buy for personal and emotional reasons, why would we take a chance turning them off by pushing too hard the first time we meet?

The best result is that the agent or broker is comfortable with you, likes you, and enjoys talking with you. Most often, that means it should not feel like a sales call, in which they feel like they are being "sold." So if you don't move beyond the interests step during your initial contact, that's fine. You're most likely *not* going to make the sale during the first encounter, so you need to make that engagement as positive and "non-selling" as you can. That's why it's so important to qualify the person during that initial contact. If you find they are truly a good connection, you will follow up with them later.

Stick with the interest step and keep them talking about what they love to do. Get their business cards and contact information and you're on your way.

DAY 93
Link to Needs: Bring Value
to the People You Meet

In the next step of the **LINK** approach, "**N**" is for needs. You need to find out your agents' or brokers' needs. This is important because they open the door for you to bring value. That's what networking is about: bringing value to the people you meet. However, you cannot ask, "So, what are some of your needs?" That would not create the type of conversational comfort you are trying to develop. Therefore, needs is often the most difficult of the four **LINK** steps to master.

Do not be surprised if you don't hear any needs the first few times you use this process. Catching needs statements is a learned skill, and your ability to listen and hear their needs will improve over time. Needs statements often occur around discussions of their lines/businesses or their interests. Listen carefully for words that suggest some of the following needs:

- Dissatisfaction in their current lines: "I've been there way too long." "We're really struggling right now." "We've just implemented a new program and it's really a mess." "Things are going well but we need to get more business for the future." "I'm trying to figure out what to do next."

- Dissatisfaction around their interests: "I'm working/traveling so much I rarely get a chance to play golf." "My weekends are so busy I rarely have a minute to myself." "I hurt my knee and I'm not able to play basketball." "I wish I could improve my golf game." "I wish I had more time to read."

- Desire to improve something with their lines: "Things are going well right now but we need to figure out how to ... " "I need to figure out how to master (a particular issue)."

- Desire to improve their interests: "My goal is to get more time at the practice range this year." "I really want to learn how to (activity) this year." "I've always wanted to go to (location)."

Because most of the needs around their lines/businesses pertain to either dissatisfaction with something or a desire to improve something, here are several questions that might keep the conversation moving:

- "What is it like working there?"

- "How do you like the role you're in?"

- "What is the next step for someone in your position?"

Since most of the needs pertain to a challenge or obstacle that's getting in the way of their interests, here are several questions you could ask:

- "How often do you get a chance to ... ?"

- "How often do you want to get out and ... ?"

- "When do you find the time to ... ?"

Keep a mental note of what you hear them say about their needs. It's important to recognize that many of their needs may have nothing to do with business. You can start relationships with many prospects by providing value not related to their business—for example, an article or note about a recreational, personal, family, or sport need. By paying attention to these needs and providing value, you begin to develop a personal and emotional bond.

It takes a long time to develop a network of referral partners. Bringing "non-business" value to others is a long-term investment. Make sure you reward these agents and brokers the same way you would reward a good referral from a satisfied customer that turns into a sale. Follow the same guidelines covered in Day 88 and you're on you way to additional agent or broker leads.

DAY 94
Link to Knowledge: Learn About What and Who They Know

Because networking and developing relationships with agents and brokers is about bringing value, then understanding a new contact's knowledge base is essential. In the **LINK** program, "**K**" is for knowledge. That understanding enables you to connect *them* to someone else in your network that needs what/whom they know.

Most contacts are more than happy to share what they know and whom they know, if given the chance. But we are usually so focused on telling everyone what we do that we never learn anything about the person we are talking with. Worse, that person walks away with a feeling that the world revolves around us and our experiences and that we don't really care about him or her.

Think about a recent business or social engagement where you met someone new, and all the person did was speak about him/herself. How did you feel about that engagement? Chances are you wanted to interject and say something about your experiences. Chances are you thought to yourself, "My gosh, does this person ever come up for air?" Maybe you thought, "This person seems quite self-centered." In most cases, you did not walk away with a warm and fuzzy feeling that this is someone you want to head out for lunch with the following day. Why? Because the conversation was totally about him/her and you wanted some airtime.

The **LINK** process helps you get the focus off you and onto the person you are speaking with. It helps create positive feelings about you so you can move forward with agents or brokers. In this situation everyone wins. They'll walk away feeling like they had a great conversation. You walk away knowing about their lines, their interests, what they need, what they know, and who they know. You'll walk away with information that can help you bring value to the prospects and possibly develop a business relationship if you identified an opportunity during the conversation.

In order to get them to share their area of knowledge, make an occasional observation when they become engaged in a topic. For instance, if they are speaking about their lines and become quite animated, you could make the observation, "It seems like you have a real passion about (their lines). Is this something you've always been interested in?" This gets the conversation going deeper around their knowledge and may even open up a connection to whom they know. Probe!

Often their knowledge results from their interests. When they become very engaged and animated about their interests, simply make the observation: "It sounds like you know a lot about … . ?" Or "How did you get so involved with … ?"

The knowledge step is the least understood and the most frequently abused of all the steps in the **LINK** process. Many salespeople try to force their way into getting names from brokers and agents in an effort to drop those same names with others in a lame attempt at networking. Who someone knows is a very personal piece of information that must be treated with extreme caution. At the same time, whom they know is often the most valuable link you will uncover.

Most often people will share the name of someone they know in the course of a conversation. It may be the name of someone they work with, a customer, a friend, or business acquaintance. If the contact mentions a name that interests you, be cautious about showing visual signs of heightened awareness. Remember, **LINK**ing is about the person you are networking with *and not about you.* Keep the conversation going without appearing self-serving. Ask, "Oh, Sally Smith. How long have you known Sally?" The length of time a contact has known a key target is a great indication of the type of true relationship they have. Find out what they know and who they know and you're on your way.

DAY 95
Accumulate LINK Information:
Make a Note of It

At each point in the **LINK** process I made the comment, "Make a mental note." If you are having this **LINK** conversation in a networking environment, it is often unacceptable to make written notes. However, there is often critical information that you must capture. I recommend using the contact's business card for that purpose.

Here's how it works. When the timing is right, make a reinforcing statement such as "It sounds like you have a great company/product" or "I've really enjoyed our conversation"—whatever is an honest and sincere statement. Then, take one of your business cards and offer it to them with the statement/request, "Here's my business card, do you have a card?" The fact that you gave them your card first creates an obligation in them to give you their card. If they do not have a card with them, then it is fine for you to say, "No problem, I have another card. Just write down your name and contact information on the back of my card." Either way you walk away with their contact information on a card.

Once you have a quiet moment write down the **LINK** information you've gathered on the back of the business card. Use one corner for line information, another corner for interest, another for needs, and the final corner for what they know and whom they know. Also write the date and where you met (the venue, association meeting, kids' softball game, specific meeting, etc.) in the center of the back of the card to make it easier for you to remember where you met.

As you continue to use the **LINK** process you will improve your ability to file away key names and issues that surface as the contact is talking. In the beginning, simply head off to another room for a minute after your conversation and jot down your notes in the format we mentioned. Over time you'll be able to keep information in your head from two to three people and then transfer it to the business cards later, away from the networking event.

The great thing about **LINK** is that it positions your future conversations. You have key information to make meaningful conversations, and you are always looking for other needs that your contacts have, along with their knowledge and who they know. Needs and know/knowledge are the two areas that will be the most dynamic over time and are often the source of the greatest connections.

DAY 96
Is In-home Sales the Right
Role for You?

The question is often asked, "How long should it take before I know whether a new salesperson is going to make it?" Sales managers wonder how long it should take before they know whether a new salesperson is going to make it or whether they should move on. It's a good question.

The answer is, "It depends, but certainly no longer than 100 days." That's not a trick answer. Regardless of the sales cycle for your product or service, when salespeople have clear plans for incremental steps in their sales processes and diligently complete the steps as set forth in the plan, that is a very good indication of how well they will do long term. The only variable is the amount of time spent on product training (i.e., if you have a six-week product training schedule before you enter the field, then the "100-day clock" starts at the end of the product training).

There are two key caveats: the company's plan/strategy for the salesperson and the follow-through by the salesperson. When a company brings on a new salesperson, it must have a clear plan and strategy to help the salesperson become successful. That's why this book was written. It's a template that a company can use to clearly measure whether the new salesperson is doing all the necessary activities and evaluate whether he or she has developed the sales skills to be successful. If you are self-employed or if your new employer does not have a clear plan/strategy to help you become successful, then it's up to you to develop the plan. Aside from the specific number of calls, proposals, or sales you must make, this book will provide you with a comprehensive plan for the first 100 days and beyond.

The second caveat is the follow-through by the salesperson. And that is why on Day 96 we are posing the question, "Is **In-home** sales the right role for you?" Be honest; how have you done over the past 95 days? Have you learned the techniques, followed the process, and been diligent about meeting your measurable goals? Have you had success when networking? Have you had success diligently prospecting? Have you uncovered qualified opportunities? Have you developed and asked great questions when on a call? Have you moved the opportunity to the next step? Have you successfully closed sales? Have you gone back and asked for referrals? *Is **In-home** sales the right role for you?*

Ultimately it does not matter what your employer thinks—it's your decision. If you believe **In-home** sales is the right role for you then you have the right attitude to become a sales professional.

For today, look back over the past 96 days at where you had success, identify your sales strengths, and write them down. See where you fell short and write down your areas for improvement. Tomorrow you will sit down with your sales manager or, if self-employed, an accountability partner and plan the future.

DAY 97
In-home Sales Mantra No. 27:
From Heroes to Zeros—
What's Your Next Move?

It's been one week since you read Mantra No. 26. Did you set aside time to practice this past week? Did you share your plan with someone and ask them to hold you accountable? If you did practice and shared your progress with your accountability partner, how was your confidence each day?

In-home salespeople are always given sales goals. They may be daily, weekly, monthly, or annual sales quota/budget goals. The budget is typically set by the owner or upper management, and it's how you will be measured by your company. Depending on how your results compare to your goals will create the up and down swing of sales. We compare it to a rollercoaster. You go high up and when you hit the top, the highest peak of the coaster, you are on top of the world.

The **In-home** salesperson feels much the same at the top. You're a hero. You have gained the respect of your peers, and on occasion others pull you into the break room and ask what you are doing to be number one. In the sales meeting your sales manager or president may commend you for your results and pump your ego. They use you as an example—a winner and a closing machine. The feeling is unexplainable, and it makes every aspect of your life better because you feel invincible. When you walk, your shoulders are broad and you feel that any prospect who crosses your path will become a customer. Wouldn't this be great if we felt this way all year long?

Logic and experience demonstrates that we can't stay at the top forever. Much like the rollercoaster, you start your descent. Your gut feels like it just left your body. As a friend of mine once said, "In sales we go from heroes to zeros." We have a good day, a good month, or a good year, and we start the next day with zero sales. Perhaps you started reading this book when things were tough from a sales standpoint. You are down and it seems very hard to get back up.

Let's say you've had a bad closing streak. Nothing is going your way. Because you need a sale to generate income, on your next appointment you smell like a fish to your prospect because you are desperate. The prospect senses this and is resistant. You're not your normal smooth self, because you will do and say anything to sell and get out of this slump. You may even find yourself skipping steps in the **In-home** Sales **Continuum**™ to hurry things along. After you missed your sales, you get in your vehicle and say to yourself, "What just happened? These people should be my customer." We call this starting from zero. No place but up!

Then there is another scenario. You just ended your month as the top sales closer. Everyone is getting you coffee because you're the top gun, the *hero*. But surprise, day one of the following month you're back to *zero*. The grind starts all over, and you want to stay at the top. You know the rest of the sales force is chasing you; they are tired of always hearing your name. Everyone wants to be a hero, not a zero. In both cases, we are starting from zero. No place but up!

If you are on top of your game, keep doing the same things from the 10 Step **In-home** Sales **Continuum**™ that got you to the top. If you are on the bottom, then embrace the 10 Step **In-home** Sales **Continuum**™. You need to do something different. Insanity is doing the same thing and expecting a different result.

Type the following statement into a computer, make the font large enough to read from a distance, and run several copies to place in your car, your Fact Finder portfolio, your professional presentation book—wherever you sit and set appointments—and the mirror in your home. Repeat it over and over again and spend more of your time as a hero versus the alternative. Remember, depending on where you are in the process you are still going from zero to being a hero.

*I will not change my proven sales system. I will execute the 10 Step **In-home** Sales **Continuum**™ regardless of my situation. I know selling is a numbers game. I know that I need to experience numerous nos to get a few yeses. <u>It's not how many times I get kicked down; IT'S HOW FAST I GET UP!</u>* By continuing to practice the 10 step In-home Sales Continuum™ you will avoid the number 1 reason In-home salespeople fail from Day 3. Congratulations!

DAY 98
In-home Sales Mantra No. 28:
It's Not How You Start,
It's How You Finish

Regardless of your "current" situation it is only that – your "current situation." Some of you have made incredible progress with the **In-home** Sales **Continuum**™ process during the previous 97 days. Some of you may have started the **In-home** process and run into challenges, obstacles, or interruptions. You started with the best of intentions but were sidetracked. The key is to determine how you will get back on track and achieve your goals.

Several years ago I decided to take up running. There is no shortage of running accessories, and I invested in all of them: running shoes, running clothes, running outerwear, running socks, running sunglasses, running gloves for the cooler weather, and running earphones for the running digital audio players. Next there were running books and training manuals meant to coach me in the right direction. Finally, there was equipment: tread mills and exercise bicycles to round out my training. I invested in all of them because I was committed to running.

None of this prepared me for the reality of how I felt once I actually started running. It was not as easy as the books, videos, and instruction manuals made it look. Although all the equipment improved my situation, running required a lot more effort and pain than I had expected. There are four things I learned quickly:

1. When I ran I found that setting incremental goals while running made it easier to achieve my final destination. Picking a landmark half a mile down the road and running to that goal was manageable. Upon meeting that incremental goal, I would select another landmark another half mile down the road. It was easier to achieve the incremental goals along the way than to look three miles down the road.

2. When I stopped I found it very difficult to restart. Once I stopped short of my goal, it was very difficult to get started running again. Much of this was mental. It was as if I had given up. Then my physical side would remind me of how nice it was to walk and be able to breathe normally. It was a false sense of satisfaction as I was no longer achieving my goal.

3. During subsequent runs I found I was prone to stop more often because I stopped during the last run. My lack of achievement reinforced my inability to get to the next level. Even when I finally finished the run there was something missing because I had stopped along the way.

4. If I set my mind to completing the run, without stopping, and persevered through the mental and physical assaults, I had a much greater sense of accomplishment, and subsequent runs became less difficult. The reinforcement that came with finishing the run and achieving my goal had positive implications far beyond simply running.

Set incremental goals as you move forward! If you made incredible progress during the past 97 days, then continue and set new incremental goals to continue to grow your sales. If you ran into challenges, obstacles, or interruptions that kept you from achieving your goals, then pick up where you left off and set incremental goals to help you get back on track. The ideas you learn today will help you overcome challenge No. 3 from Day 3: managing your time.

Keep going! Recognize that every time you stop it is much more difficult to get back on track. Status quo is not possible with human development. You are either moving forward or going in reverse. When you keep moving forward, you are moving in the right direction. Once you start, keep going!

When you accomplish a goal, reinforce yourself! By reinforcing your accomplishment you increase the probability of succeeding in similar endeavors in the future. *Whatever you reinforce you get more of,* so reinforce your incremental accomplishments and you'll begin to attract even greater success.

Take time today to reinforce the accomplishments you've already made and make the commitment to:

- Set incremental goals going forward

- Keep going regardless of the challenges

- Continually reinforce yourself with each accomplishment.

DAY 99
Setting a Positive Course
for the Future

On Day 96 we mentioned that sales managers often ask us, "How long should it take before I know whether the new salesperson is going to make it?" Today you're going to be proactive and answer the question for your sales manager. Even if you have been in sales for many years with your company, you owe it to yourself to take this step with your sales manager.

It's best to make mid-course corrections sooner rather than later before your challenges become bad habits. It's been roughly three months since you started this process. On Day 96 you wrote your list of successes and your strengths. You also wrote down your challenges and the areas where you need to improve. Now it's time to sit down with your sales manager and share your findings. If **In-home** sales is the right role for you, then now is the time to get his or her commitment to your continued success. Here are the items to cover:

- The sales manager's expectations. Whatever plan you were given or expectations that were placed upon you when you started should be reviewed.

- Your results. Review your progress with regard to the plans and expectations given to you by your sales manager. This begins to build his or her confidence in your abilities.

- Your recent effort. Share the work you have done over the past 100 days with the techniques, processes, and skills in the book. This reinforces that you are a self-motivated and self-disciplined sales professional.

- Your strengths and how to leverage. Review your list of strengths and ask your sales manager whether he/she agrees with your observations. Dig and probe to make sure you are in agreement. Now spend a few minutes talking about how best to leverage your strengths going forward. This informs your sales manager of your strengths and builds their confidence in your value to the sales team.

- Your areas for improvement and how to address them. Review your list of challenges and the areas of improvement you've identified. Ask your sales manager whether he/she agrees with your observations. Dig and probe to make sure you are in agreement. Identify several options for how to improve in each area that you need to work on. This shows your sales manager you are self-aware of your challenges and you are actively working to improve in those areas.

- Go-forward plan and time frame. Finally, do not leave without a plan and a time frame. Here are a few tips to use during this step so your plans/goals will help you succeed:

  — Make certain whatever you agree with is clearly understood by both you and your sales manager.

  — Make certain each item can be measured. Ask yourself the question, "How will I know I have met this expectation?"

  — Is this goal reasonable? Has anyone ever attained this before? Would your sales manager be willing to agree to this goal if he or she were in your position?

— Will the achievement of this goal make a difference to your sales? Set plans that drive sales volume.

— There needs to be a date when each agreed-upon step in the plan will be completed.

Now you have support from your sales manager and a clear plan to continue your success. You've begun to master challenge No. 14 from Day 3: continuing your sales education. Continue to evaluate your progress and gain additional selling skills through further sales education and you will always be on top of your game. Continue to go to www.salesoctane.com and hit In-home sales for additional offerings and insights for the In-home sales professional.

Congratulations!

Sell Smart and Sell More!

DAY 100
Notes for Your Sales Leader

If you are a sales manager, sales coach, or maybe even a curious owner reading this book, I want to pass on my seven key points. Embrace each of the points and your sales will soar.

1. *Have a sales system in place.* The basis of this book has been the 10 Step **In-home** Sales **Continuum**™. If you don't have a system in place to drive each step with your salespeople, you will not be able to gauge sales performance. The **In-home** Sales **Continuum**™ is like a chain; if one link breaks, the whole chain is useless. Your job is to find the break and repair it. You must reinforce the **In-home** Sales **Continuum**™ each week in your sales meetings, as well as every time you ride with a salesperson.

2. *Gain your sales teams respect early.* Don't place yourself in a jeopardizing situation. As a sales manager, I always refused the bar offers as I wanted to keep our relationship at a business level. If you keep your reputation as a professional, you will gain your sales teams respect as a sales leader. Telling nasty jokes or making fun of other people diminishes your credibility as a person and as a sales manager. Invest in your sales knowledge by listening to CDs and reading sales periodicals. That way, when your salespeople ride with you, they will see that you practice what you preach.

3. *Hold them accountable.* I have always spot-checked salespeople in meetings by calling out a step in the 10 Step **In-home** Sales **Continuum**™ and asking one of them to share the techniques used in that step. Role-play during your sales meetings and practice, drill, and rehearse each step in the system. Once a salesperson sees another sales representative getting called on in a sales meeting, he or she will not want to be embarrassed the following week if he/she gets called on to role-play in a similar situation. Keep in mind, we are not role-playing to make people look foolish. Our goal is to hold them accountable through coaching.

Let's say you are in a sales meeting with 15 sales representatives. Jerry is a new sales rep who has been employed with you for three months. The topic of discussion at the meeting is asking the prospect for the order and handling objections. Tell Jerry that he just delivered a price to a prospect of $14,650 for a new addition, and the customer responded, "I need to think about it; leave me your business card and I will get back to you." Ask Jerry what he would do next. If Jerry does a poor job, simply reinforce him for the one thing he did well, even if it's simply breathing, and tell him it's OK. Ask him to do it again and prime him with some thoughts. Ask others in the group for suggestions but keep bringing it back to Jerry until he does a good role-play. At that point reinforce him by telling him he did a good job and you have confidence in him. Later, after the meeting, talk to Jerry in private and reinforce the importance of practice.

Have your salespeople show you their designs, pricing, and completed Fact Finders from sales calls and praise them for the areas where they have done good jobs. This way you can make sure they are doing each of the steps at a level that will make you proud. The minute you get lazy reviewing each step in the process with each of them you will find their performances slipping.

BONUS TIPS

4. Be firm but fair. Your salespeople will respect you more when they see that you are firm but fair. You will always be tested by your team members to see what you will do in any given situation. If you were once one of the salespeople and now you are managing your former peers, you have a significant challenge. Never lose your temper or show anger. Never show stress. These people look up to you, and if you have a bad day and are stressed and lash out, then it will impact how they see you in the future. If you start getting negative, then they feel it's acceptable to be negative . If you have a specific need in this area contact us at www.salesoctane.com and select In-home products and service and ask about our leadership programs.

5. *Their income makes your income.* When salespeople know that their sales manager, coach, or owner is looking out for their best interests, they will jump through flaming hoops for that leader. For instance, if you see a possible charge back of lost commission for one of your salespeople and you bring that person into your office and go to war for him or her, that salesperson will tell others, and respect starts to grow. Remember, if they sell more, you make more. Fight for them.

6. *Lead by example.* How you dress, your language, and the way you carry yourself is under evaluation by your salespeople. At one time in my **In-home** selling career, at the age of 26, I had over 100 sales representatives working for me. At that time I also had five district managers reporting to me. I wore the best clothes I could buy and was noted for my elaborate ties. I bought a Jaguar convertible and made around $2,500 a week average (this was great money 20 years ago). When you're at the top, people want to hang with you, be you, and talk to you. They want to pick your brain to under-

stand how to close more business. All this is fine as long
as you watch what you say and how you say it. There was
one reason why I drove that car and dressed the way I did.I
wanted the reps to see what they could have if they achieved
their sales goals.

7. *Invest in your salespeople and they will invest in you.* In 1992 I left
another state to move home to be with my father after my
mother passed away. I took a job as an **In-home** sales representative selling residential security systems. I had some
early success with the sales process as I was the only one who
followed a sales system. The owner of the company eventually sold out and retired. One day he called me and asked
me to have lunch with him. During lunch he let me know
how much he appreciated me and all my sales efforts. He
noticed that my shoes were a bit worn. I told him it was from
the amount of walking I had to do to hit my sales call goals
and that they were not that expensive so it was fine. After
lunch he stopped at a high-end shoe store and much to my
surprise asked me to try on a pair of very expensive shoes.
He asked how they felt. I replied that it was like walking
on pillows but I was not in a position to spend over $300
for a pair of shoes. He replied, "Ron, you need to understand that these shoes actually come with a blueprint and
you can send them back to get reconstructed whenever they
become worn, so you will have them for life." I again said
that it sounded good but I was planning to stay with the $69
shoes and replace them once a year. He asked me again if I
liked the expensive shoes, to which I replied, "I love them."
He responded by handing the salesman his credit card and
bought me the shoes. From that day on I told myself that
I would not only sell for this guy, but I would go over and

beyond my sales budget. It is 2009 and I still own those shoes, and they are in near mint condition.

Lead by example, treat your salespeople fairly and reinforce the proven 10 step In-home Sales Continuum™. Coach them to sell smart and they will sell more!

Jim Ryerson

Ron Kahoun

APPENDIX A-1
Ben Franklin Close

This is one of my favorite closing techniques and I have used it consistently over the past 20 years. The reason it works is because the close is very logical. We know that at times we might have to ask for the order three to five times. We know that most people need to be asked repeatedly, and around the fourth to fifth attempt it all makes sense to them and they are ready to move forward. Sadly most sales people might ask once and leave. This is due to lack of training, fear of rejection, or feeling like they are too pushy. This close is best used around the fourth to fifth attempt.

Prospect: "Well, Ron, I appreciate all you have done and just give us a couple of days to decide and we will call you back."

In-home sales pro: "John, I appreciate that. It sounds like you need a couple of days to weigh the facts of why to make this purchase or maybe not to."

Prospect: "Yes, that's pretty much what we are going to do."

In-home sales pro: "John, you're just like me. When my wife and I need to make a major purchase, we do the same—we weigh the facts. Before I leave, if you don't mind, may I show you what my wife and I do that makes a lot of sense?"

Prospect: "Sure."

In-home sales pro: "Have you ever heard of Ben Franklin?"

Prospect: "Yes we have."

In-home sales pro: "Ben was in the same situation many of times that you're in right now. Ben created a very simple system. Grab a sheet of paper and pencil real quick. Now, take this sheet of paper and draw a horizontal line at the top and a vertical line right down the middle. On the left side write the word YES, and on the left side write the word NO. Let's start with the left side."

Ask him, for example, if he liked:

- Your company warranties

- You

- Your product

- Your product's material and craftsmanship

- Your design

- Your product's colors and options

- That you have been around over 25 years.

Try to get at least 15 yeses, and, when you get them, place a check mark under the YES column.

In-home sales pro: "Great, now on the left side (NO column, and hand them the pen and let them write the answer), write down all the reasons why you don't want the new deck; for example maybe the price?"

Prospect: "Yes, I would say that is one reason. We really can't think of any others."

YES	NO
✔ Did you like me?	Did you like the price/payment? ✔
✔ Did you like my company?	
✔ Did you Like my product?	
✔ Did you like the time frame For install?	
✔ Did you like that we have in-house Installers?	
✔ Did you like our written warranties?	
✔ Did you like that we are in business Over 25 years?	
✔ Did you like we are fully insured?	
8 Yes	**1 NO**

In-home sales pro: "Great John, we have 17 reasons why to buy and 1 no. Doesn't it make sense to move forward when the facts state this is a good decision? Let me confirm your address."

APPENDIX A-2
Higher Authority Close

If in the event you have made three or four attempts to close, this technique will really unveil if the customer is stalling or just trying to get rid of you. The key is to follow the exact steps.

In-home sales pro: "John, I am on my way and I appreciate the time that we spent." (By saying you are about to leave brings a sigh of relief and the temperature down.)

Prospect: "Ron, you have been great, give me a week and I will get back to you."

In-home sales pro: "Sounds good. John, before I go, I would like to grade my performance. I know you need to think about it and you have informed me that I was $1,500 higher than my nearest competitor. You have in good faith shown me the competitor's bid, and I see we are very close in product and design. But I sensed you felt we were a better company."

Prospect: "I did, I felt you were more professional, but $1,500 is a lot of money." (It's a must here that the customer admits you have a better company and product.)

In-home sales pro: "It sure is, but you do see why we are more, right?"

Prospect: "I do." (The key is the customer admits that he/she sees why your price is more and the added value.)

In-home sales pro: "Well I did the best I could, but before I go, let me ask you: Had I been able to match or even gotten closer to the competitor's bid, you most likely would have given me the go-ahead, wouldn't you?"

Prospect: "Probably, I guess. Are you saying you can?" (You must get a commitment here or the close won't work.)

In-home sales pro: "Well John, I can't. I gave you my best, but hang tight. I may know someone that can help me out that is higher up than me." (Saying "John, I can't" is the take-away. Also note that by saying you can't give John a better price, you're holding your credibility. If you were to drop the price here, the customer might ask himself why he didn't ask for more money off the original price.)

Next, make the call to your sales manager. Also make sure you have $1,500 of room or can get close without going in the red. Remember these words: You can always go down but you can't go up! By calling someone of higher authority it makes you appear you're on the prospect's side and you're willing to give it all away just to gain a customer. Also, you must practice this technique with your sales manager or the person of higher authority you're calling so you don't throw them off guard.

APPENDIX A-3
Reduce to Pennies Close:
Overcoming the Price Objection

This closing technique is used when you want to demonstrate to your prospect how small the investment will be by breaking down the investment into a very small increment.

Prospect: "Well Ron, when we're ready, we will most likely go the cash route. But I think we need to *think about it.* (At this point, pause, let what he said echo in his brain It might even sound silly after he thinks about it.)

In-home sales pro: "Sure John, that's not the first time in my career I have heard that statement. If you're like me you probably need a few days. Today is Thursday; you mostly likely need until Saturday, I mean you are going to (remodel X, build X), right?" (By saying you have heard this before says that others feel the same way; the prospect is not an oddball. Saying "you're like me" creates empathy. Notice you say a few days, not weeks or months. At the end you're confirming that the prospect wants the product; if not, why even go further? After hearing the price, the prospect may say he is broke and can't afford it.)

Prospect: "Oh yes, we are definitely going to (remodel X, build X). We just need a few days. It's a big investment, and Sara and I need to talk it over." (This is normal. Who wouldn't want to think about $1,425? That could be a new TV.)

In-home sales pro: "Tell you what I am going to do. All of these notes are for my files. Let me draw up a quick copy for you so you have something to review the next couple of days. That way you can make a good sound decision." (This buys you time. By indicating that you are leaving you brought the pressure down and the prospect feels relieved.)

Prospect: "Perfect, do you need another cup of coffee?" (He makes this offer because you are a nice person, polite and you respect that he needs a few days.)

In-home sales pro: "Please, one more cup for the road." (Four minutes goes by.) "John, before I leave I wanted to make sure I did a good job tonight, kind of grade myself, and make sure I didn't miss anything. I know you have some thinking to do. Was it the design? (You're back in control by asking questions again.)

Prospect: "No, Ron, the design is perfect. Maybe a little over-kill but it is the dream X." (You know that's not the problem, but, of course, you confirmed the design in Step 8 before you delivered the price in Step 9.)

In-home sales pro: "I felt that you and Sara really liked that design. Was it me or my company that you needed to think about?"

Prospect: "Oh gosh no, you were fun and very informing. In fact, you blew away the last guy that was here. We feel you did a great job." (You just found out or confirmed they have another bid.)

In-home sales pro: "Thanks John, I also felt that we connected. I believe strongly that you and Sara feel comfortable with the stability of my company and products. John, would it be fair to assume that the price came in a bit more than you were expecting?" (Don't pause here.) "I mean we're at $16,425 with the special discounts. Did you feel it would be $16,000 or $16,200? (Time to unveil the smokescreen. Notice the small difference amount. If you have said $10,000, how would you have made up the $6,425? John might have said, "Yes, we were hoping it would be only $10,000.")

Prospect: "Well, yes, it's a bit more. We thought or were hoping it would be around $15,000." (When you get this answer, you're 90 percent home. All they wanted to do was compare the difference over the weekend.)

In-home sales pro: "I understand. Actually, we're not that far apart—only $1,425. Was the number $15,000 based on anything factual like a newspaper ad or another bid, or was it just a hope number?" (Again you understand, $1,425 is now an isolated number and you found out it's compared to another bid, not a hope number.)

Prospect: "It was the guy before you, ABC Inc."

In-home sales pro: "Oh yes, I am familiar with them. Well this makes me feel much better. You like me, my superior company and product, but what you needed to think about was the $1,425 difference. $1,425 is a large amount of money. My suggestion would be since I am an expert in this field and I happen to be here right now let's get out the other proposal and make sure they are at least apples and apples as far as options. I could do this at a glance." (Now the moment of truth: Are they lying, was there really another bid, or were they trying to politely get rid of you? If they show you this bid, you're now 95 percent home.)

Prospect: "Well, um, er. . . I am not sure we need to do that right now. I can dig it out and look at them both over the weekend." (You can't accept that; the emotional level is high.)

In-home sales pro: "Yes you can, but since you agreed earlier that you were going to get (the product or service you are selling), and I am a trusted professional, it makes sense to compare the two while I am here. That way, if anything confuses you, I can have an immediate answer. This makes sense, wouldn't you agree?" (Notice the tie-down at the end. If they say no here, there is no other bid and they want to dismiss you.)

Prospect: "Well, OK then. Sara, can you run over to the kitchen and grab that bid from the other day?" (John feels maybe you are right, maybe he needs to get an expert to review this with him. He does not want the pain of trying to make a decision on his own and having to reread the bids and try to remember the features and benefits of each on his own.)

In-home sales pro: "Well, John, it seems that the bids are identical as far as size and options, but the quality of the labor and material will be the difference. Before I go, I have one final question: Indeed, we are $1,425 apart, but do you and Sara see the difference in the quality of material, craftsmanship, and companies?" (They may or may not be the same in options. If not, that's easy to address. What's important in this step is getting them to confirm the quality of your product so they can see why you cost more. If they can't, you messed up Step 6 and did not build enough value.)

Prospect: "Oh with no doubt, your product is way better. You don't use subs and your company is more solid. Also I like you better. The problem is it's still $1,425 and I need to justify that." (They just bought you; now you need to justify the $1,425.)

In-home sales pro: "You remind me of myself. My wife and I just went through the same process when it came to remodeling our basement. I went out and got three bids. You lay the three bids on the table, and, of course, you have the low, middle, and high one. Most people throw out the low one, thinking it's too cheap and my family deserves better. The high one you throw out because you feel the middle bid is safe. In this case you will agree here that I am $1,425 higher, but at least you know why, don't you?" (Tell a true story to demonstrate that you also feel their pain. What they are thinking is normal. And, most importantly, they agree and confirm they know why you're more expensive. Again notice the tie-down in the end.)

Prospect: "Of course, product and labor."

In-home sales pro: "John and Sara, earlier you told me you lived here five years and that you likely will be here 15 to 20 more." (Hand them a calculator.) "Could you please punch these numbers in for me, Sara: $1,425 over 20 years = $71.25 year, divided by 12 months equal = $5.94 per month, divided by 30 = 20 cents per day. This sounds kind of ridiculous but for 20 cents a day you can have peace of mind with this product backed by a solid company and written warranty. It makes sense doesn't it?"

Prospect: "Yes it does."

In-home sales pro: "This home is located at 123 Water Lane?"

(Assume the sale.)

APPENDIX A-4
How to Close When You Get the
"I Need to See My Banker" Objection

I find in my travels in coaching and on-site training that a high majority of new salespeople walk away from a sale when the prospect says, "Sounds good. We need to go see our banker." When you allow this, you are in jeopardy of losing your sale. Once you let them go, you lose all contact and control. You may run into a situation where the banker knows another contractor and can give your prospect a better deal. *This cannot happen.* This is why I stress having financing available. At times you will get prospects that want a better interest rate or even apply for a home equity loan. The key is to get the agreements signed and get at least 5 to 10 percent down.

You need to make sure this not a stall or that they are just trying to get rid of you.

In-home sales pro: "Fantastic, so John what you are saying is that you need to go to your banker and get the funds arranged, and when you do you will get back with me because XYZ Decking is the company for you?"

Prospect: "Yes, that is correct. Leave me your card and I will call you when the arrangements are made."

In-home sales pro: "Not a problem, John. You have confirmed that XYZ Decking is for you. Let me tell you from my experience that most bankers need proper documents for the loan arrangement. What we need to do is complete the written agreement and you can give me as little as X amount down, then I will return to get the remaining amount after you receive the funds. Let me confirm your address again."

Prospect: "Sure, it's 123 Water Lane."

When you leave without a signed agreement and the prospects have a price, you have now put yourself in a jeopardizing situation of having a competitor steal your sale from you. Remember, if you don't close your sale, you don't make any money.

APPENDIX A-5
The 1-10 Close

Here is another type of close. Once you're at the moment of truth, ask this question to obtain the order of information or the level of commitment you need to get the order.

In-home sales pro: "Mr. Jones, on a scale of 1 to 10, with 10 meaning you're ready to move forward, where would you stand right now?"

Prospect: "I would say I am about an 8."

In-home sales pro: "I sensed you were at an 8. The difference between an 8 and a 10 is not very much. OK, Mr. Jones, you're at an 8. What would it take to move you to a 10?"

Prospect: "Well, maybe a better price."

If you get a 7 or below, you have blown Steps 3 through 8.

APPENDIX A-6
Take away close

You should use this closing technique first if possible. After you convert the "No" to "We need to think about it", or you get the "We need to think about it" right away then use the below script:

- I will start you from the last part of the "We need to think about it script".

In-home sales pro: "OK, John, I understand. One question before I leave: Earlier, when I asked you, other than price, could I earn your business (step 7/day 57), you replied, 'I don't see any other reason, and based on that **it can't be me or my company.** Would it be fair to assume the price came in a bit more than you were expecting?" (Don't pause here.) "I mean, I was at $15,250. Did you think it was going to come in at around $15,000 even?" (Don't give yourself a huge price gap here, and then shut up!)

Prospect: "Well, yes, it was more than we thought; we were expecting it to be around $14,000."

In-home sales pro: "Great, we are not that far apart. Was that based on anything factual like a magazine article or another bid?"

Prospect: No, just what we were hoping for.

In-home sales pro: Sure, Let me ask you if my product/service was at $14,000, would you have moved forward?

Prospect: Probably. (You must get a commitment here or the technique wont work)

In-home sales pro: Great, what part of the design did you want to take away so we can get to the $14,000 range?

Its here were you will find if they were just trying to get rid of you or they are serious buyers. They may say lets take a look at the design, or they may say "no, we don't want to take away anything, we like the design the way it is". If they look at the design, make the take away and get closer to the desired price that fits them. If they don't want to make any changes then you did a good job. Now you have to sell the value gap of $14,000 to $15,250. The last option could be to lock them down on a number in between and do a higher authority close (A2) or maybe reduce to pennies (A3).

The key is not to give up and understand that it could take two- to five attempts to get the "yes". Also keep in mind not pressure the prospect, if they sense you are they will resist and you have zero chances of closing.

Jim Ryerson

 Jim Ryerson is Founder and President of Sales Octane, Inc., a group of individuals dedicated to helping others apply time-honored sales principles to grow themselves and their business. Jim started his selling career with Herman Miller, Inc., one of America's most admired corporations. Ranked as one of the top 25 sales forces in the country by *Sales and Marketing Magazine*, Jim developed several selling models during his time with Herman Miller, Inc. Jim was President of Herman Miller Workplace Resource, a distributor of office furniture and healthcare products in Northeast Ohio with annual sales of $15 million employing 52 team members. Jim has been a member and board member of Young Entrepreneurs and the world Entrepreneurs Organization for seven years and is a frequent speaker on the entrepreneurial circuit. Jim's first book, *First 100 Days of Selling*, published by WBusiness Books, is in its second printing.

Ron Kahoun

 Ron Kahoun started his in-home selling career in 1986 selling wood decks for Sears. His entire career involved techniques to ensure a one-call close. Ron has been a sales representative, regional marketing director and sales manager throughout his career. He has more than 20 years in sales/sales management experience and 17 years selling inside the home. He has several national sales awards as well as numerous record-breaking years in selling and coaching/training. Ron is a national sales coach, traveling the country coaching/training and teaching the art of In-home sales. Ron currently coaches a national sales force of more than 145 specialists hitting sales in 2008 of $110 million.

THIS BOOK DOESN'T END
AT THE LAST PAGE!

We want to hear from you!

Register your book at:
www.WBusinessBooks.com to receive
the latest business news and information.

You can communicate with the author
or share your thoughts about this book
with other members of the WBusiness
community

WBusinessBooks.com is a place where
you can sharpen your skills, learn the
new trends and network with other professionals.